MAKING MILLIONS...
INSTRUCTIONS INCLUDED

By
George L. Morgan

The Morgan Publishing Empire
Omaha, NE

Copyright © 2000 by George Morgan. All rights reserved.

No part of this work covered by the copyright hereon
may be reproduced or used in any form or by any means – graphic,
electronic, or mechanical, including photographing, recording,
taping, or information storage and retrieval systems –
without written permission of the publisher.

Morgan, George L.   1943-
Making Millions: Instructions Included

ISBN: 0-9703866-0-5

Printed in the United States of America   10   9   8   7   6   5   4   3   2   1

PUBLISHED BY:
THE MORGAN PUBLISHING EMPIRE
P.O. Box 390513
Omaha, NE 68139

ACKNOWLEDGEMENTS

When I started this project, I assumed that I would do a little research, get my thoughts down on paper, and have a book done in no time. I can assure you that this was a very, very long way from the truth. Throughout the process of this project I learned a great deal about the individuals who served as inspiration for the book, about life, and about myself. I would like to publicly thank a number of people who have not only helped me with this endeavor but who have taught me some valuable life lessons along the way. I would also like to thank them for their continued effort because the story of Making Millions is far from over.

One of the individuals who has been with me since the project's inception is Nancy O'Brien. Nancy is a native Omahan, a business consultant, and a member of the Board of Regents of the University of Nebraska system. Not only does Nancy have a significant amount of energy, she possesses a significant amount of knowledge of the Omaha community. She knows who they are and what they are and she has been involved in many of the community's recent significant events. Brian Zahm, my business partner, has been with me since I started the project and was very helpful in gathering information. Brian has also been very supportive and helped me keep my focus on the work, insisting that I "never give up the ship." Don't take this in a negative fashion, but our difference in age has proved to be invaluable to me. Brian's view of the world is considerably different than mine and he has invited me to try things that I would never have done on my own. I would also like to mention two other associates, Brian ("Mikey") Dewhurst and Gary King. Though they are recent additions to the team, I feel that they will play instrumental roles in the project as it goes forward.

I would also like to mention the father and son team of Harold and Dave Andersen. Harold is the retired editor of the *Omaha World-Herald* and he is a fine gentleman with a wealth of Omaha knowledge and he has been more than generous with his thoughts, insight, and time. Dave has provided me with a great deal of encouragement.

Bob Riley, a retired Creighton University journalism professor, provided me with great advice about the writing process and was extremely helpful whenever I got the dreaded writers' block. He knew what to do in order to get me writing. Andy Kilpatrick, a stockbroker from Birmingham, Alabama has written what has to be the definitive work on Warren Buffett called *"Permanent Value."* I have known him for at least a decade and he is an excellent role model who showed me what it takes to stay focused and to successfully complete a book.

I am also indebted to Peter Lahti, the former Chief Executive Officer and President of Kirkpatrick Pettis. Peter was extremely helpful to me in writing this book and conducting my business. Peter's insight allowed me to do some things that did not fit the usual mold of a brokerage firm. I am very grateful to him and wish him nothing but continued success. I would also like to mention two other members of the Kirkpatrick Pettis family, Lori Anderson and Ruth Sterba. They were very helpful and consistently encouraging as I worked on the book.

Several members of the community were very generous in sharing their time and knowledge. Earl Taylor was the Executive Director of the Omaha Community Foundation and spent many years researching the wealth factor in Omaha. In his position, he sought charitable giving funds and examined the ways in which those funds could be distributed throughout the community in the most advantageous ways. Early on, Earl pointed me in directions that I would never have discovered on my own. I would also like to mention Nick Taylor of the law firm of Fitzgerald, Schorr, Barmettler and Brennan. Nick's knowledge of the legal ins and outs of Omaha's charitable trusts is truly expansive. Kenny Rosen, the definitive expert on Ak-Sar-Ben, provided me with historical insights that I could not have found anywhere else. Kenny is the owner of Sir Winston, Ltd. He has been instrumental in allowing me to retain the same fashion look that I have had for the last 45 years. When Kenny decides to hang up his tailor's chalk, I'm afraid I will have to go about in trash bags.

I also need to mention the Wall Street financial media. They should not consider this a compliment. Some of my motivation for writing this book comes indirectly from them because their view of the world of finance is one sided. To them, there is only one approach to the financial world and the pin indicating the center of finance is in lower Manhattan. One of my motivations for completing this work is to show the rest of the world an alternative view of finance where the pace is significantly different, the rewards can be fairly dramatic, and the environment is nothing like the movie *Wall Street* would have you believe.

In contrast to the financial media of Wall Street, I would like to mention and compliment Omaha video and print media. They have always approached me for my view as opposed to seeking out an opinion that would only serve to support their view. In this context, I would be remiss if I did not mention Jim Rasmussen, a former business reporter for the *Omaha World-Herald* who recently left journalism to enter the Lutheran Seminary. He provided me with a great deal of insight about the skills required for effective reporting within the community. One cannot know Mr. Rasmussen without being thoroughly impressed with his integrity. I wish him nothing but the finest success as he completes his road to the ministry.

Special thanks goes to Kathleen Sullivan. The life lesson she taught me was that in order to produce a quality product you must devote the time and effort necessary to complete every detail and that a project of this nature cannot be rushed.

Last but not least, I would like to thank the members of the Omaha Financial community about whom this book is written. They have provided me with the role models for conducting my business and leading a public life. I would also like to thank the individuals in this group who were so generous with their time. I am grateful for the opportunity to hear of their philosophies and values. They have made the city I call home a better place to live.

*To Tina, Adam and Heather,
They accept me as I am.*

George

TABLE OF CONTENTS

ACKNOWLEDGEMENTS **7**

FOREWARD **15**

CHAPTER 1 .... **19**
    MR. FRANOVICH

CHAPTER 2 .... **23**
    WHAT IS A MILLIONAIRE?

CHAPTER 3 .... **31**
    HOW A COMPANY MAKES ASSETS GROW

CHAPTER 4 .... **47**
    STARTING FROM SCRATCH

CHAPTER 5 .... **51**
    THE PEOPLE OF THE
    OMAHA FINANCIAL COMMUNITY

CHAPTER 6 .... **79**
    OLD GUARD/NEW GUARD

CHAPTER 7 .... **89**
    PUBLIC AND PRIVATE

CHAPTER 8 .... **99**
    FOR THE LOVE OF THE GAME

CHAPTER 9 .... **105**
    LIFESTYLES

CHAPTER 10 .... **113**
    WHY OMAHA?

CHAPTER 11 .... **127**
    GIVING BACK TO THE COMMUNITY

CHAPTER 12 .... **137**
    CONCLUSION

FOREWARD

My association with George Morgan goes back more than 25 years. We first met at the Purdue University Krannert Graduate School of Management in West Lafayette, Indiana. Both George and I were studying and teaching in the Economics Department there. The program was one of the most rigorous and mathematical in the country. I think George realized fairly early on that he did not want to spend the rest of his life pouring over proofs and theorems and that what he really enjoyed was teaching the application of these academic ideas.

Our association at Purdue lasted about two years and from there we both went on to teaching positions in different parts of the country. George went to Ball State University in Muncie, Indiana and I took a position at Florida International University in Miami. Our paths crossed again about five years later when I moved to Omaha to take a position in the Economics Department at the University of Nebraska at Omaha. We became reacquainted through frequent lunches and discussing the various aspects of the career paths we had chosen. While I had remained in academia, George had entered the financial services industry dealing primarily with private investors. George still kept a foot in the academic world by teaching investment classes at local colleges and guest lecturing in my classes on occasion.

A few years later, George told me about a project he was working on that involved the financial community of Omaha. By this time I had taken a new position in the Finance Department at the University of Nebraska, Lincoln and I was most intrigued with his ideas. I agreed to participate in the project primarily as a sounding board for the concepts and an informal reviewer for the material he was writing.

Initially George's academic background dominated the tone of the project and he did a significant amount of statistical work on the economic and financial environment in Omaha. After a time, the orientation of the project changed considerably when he realized that his target audience was not academic and his findings about the Omaha business community had some profound personal aspects. These included the commonality of the belief system, approaches to life and the manner in which these business individuals conducted themselves. George's career in the investment area contributed greatly to his ability to personally visit with and understand these individuals.

I have witnessed the evolution of this project and hope that you will find the reading as interesting as I do. While the book focuses on the Omaha community, George's message can be applied anywhere. Read and enjoy!

Gordon V. Karels, Ph.D.
Associate Dean and Professor of Banking
Nebraska Bankers Association College
College of Business Administration
University of Nebraska, Lincoln

MAKING MILLIONS...
INSTRUCTIONS INCLUDED

By
George L. Morgan

CHAPTER 1: MR. FRANOVICH

As a teenager, I became fascinated with millionaires. The term suggested a level of wealth that was far beyond anything I could imagine, let alone acquire. I believed that millionaires led lives of freedom and glamour, unfettered by the need to save or be concerned about money. I was willing to entertain the possibility that this belief might not be true, but continued to hold fast to the notion that millionaires were, at their very essence, different from the rest of us.

I took a job at a local men's clothing store. The other employees would often make reference to the chain's owner, a man by the name of Mr. Franovich. Eventually, I learned that he was a millionaire. I couldn't wait to meet Mr. Franovich. I expected him to embody the mysterious aura of millionaire, to be recognizably different. Then I met him.

Much to my surprise, Mr. Franovich turned out to be a regular person. Suffice to say, I was a bit disappointed. Perhaps Ernest Hemingway was right. When an acquaintance of the writer suggested that the rich were somehow different than average folks, he responded with typical Hemingway simplicity. "Yeah, they have more money," he said. After meeting Mr. Franovich, my misconceptions about the wealthy began to diminish, and in their place, much deeper questions arose. What is the secret to amassing great wealth? What is the key?

These questions continued to plague me over the years. I thought about it often and observed that some people were able to gather money and make their assets grow geometrically, and, of course, other people could not. I began to consider the possibility that people who were skilled with money had somehow, somewhere, stumbled upon the fundamental instructions for turning money into wealth. I assumed that these instructions were carefully guarded secrets to which only a select few had access.

I began my career as an economics professor and after ten years of studying and teaching the operations of money, I was still not privy to the secret instructions of the wealthy. I did not find the secret to wealth in the academic environment because real wealth is not about formulae and mathematics. I left teaching and began my work in the financial services industry in Omaha, initially with a Savings and Loan. From the perspective of customers' savings accounts, Omaha did not appear to be the least bit unusual because at the Savings and Loan, significant wealth was not wholly visible. Several years later I transferred to a securities firm and gradually my view of Omaha began to change.

The more involved I became in Omaha's financial industry, the more I realized that there were a great number of people in Omaha who had apparently found the secret of making money. My curiosity about wealth expanded then to include questions of geography and community. I began to believe that the economic environment of Omaha was somehow responsible for the wealth of these individuals, and I did a great deal of research on Omaha's economic environment. (Please refer to the Appendix for some of these interesting facts.) But upon closer study, I wondered if Omaha's economic environment was exceptional *because* of its wealthy residents. As I got to know some of these people, the pieces began to slowly come together. I was determined to make a study of these folks and thereby discover the secret instructions for making money.

Over the next several years I did just that. I researched their businesses. I observed them at work and at play. I followed their activity in the community. With this foundation, I slowly began to discover the elusive instructions for gathering wealth. At the time, I was teaching some investment classes at Metropolitan Community College, so I set out to create a framework of the instructions that I could apply toward my classes. With much enthusiasm, I got the instructions down on paper and took a look at it. Once again, I found myself perplexed. "This can't be it," I said. "This is just too simple. Too easy." There was nothing complex in the framework I had created. No deep, dark secrets. No private, clever tactics. I thought, "If this is all there is to it, these simple, trivial guidelines, then everyone would be wealthy." I felt as though the process of gaining wealth had eluded me again. I relegated my elementary framework to the shelf and went back to my business.

Then, about three years ago, I found myself in a position where I might get to the heart of the matter. Several opportunities arose for me to talk with some of these very wealthy people. From our conversations, I would gather the secrets, the real instructions. I began making phone calls. I explained my intention to write a book on the creation of wealth and was pleased and surprised to discover how many people were willing and eager to share their stories with me.

What became immediately clear to me was that these people were not interested in telling me how much they were worth. Rather, they told me about their backgrounds, their lives, their values and philosophies. It was clear to me that all of these pieces were integral factors in their accumulation of wealth. I began to recognize a common thread in all of my discussions. The creation of wealth is made possible by a few simple things: hard work, perseverance, faith in yourself and your vision, faith in your company, investing in yourself and your company, and patience.

Once again, I found these answers too simple. These local millionaires were not merely prosperous. They were beyond prosperous. They had created a great deal of wealth in the arena of hundreds of millions through businesses they started or acquired. As I examined these people in the context of the greater community, I began to identify a symbiotic relationship between these Omaha millionaires and the community as a whole.

My position in an investment company gave me the opportunity to obtain information about both publicly held and privately held companies. I knew that Omaha had a lot of wealth, but the more I researched, the more I realized that the means by which this wealth was accumulated differed greatly from my previously held notions. I was tapping into Omaha's rich and unusual history and was eager to share the story with others.

After starting this book I was invited to speak for several service groups such as the Rotary Club and the Optimists. I was surprised to learn how little the younger members of the business community knew about the history of their city. When I spoke to service groups whose membership rules required that the member be 65 or older, my experience was entirely different. The members knew the history of their city and held it in high esteem. They had gone to school with Omaha's financial elite and had shared a wide variety of life experiences with them. It was clear that this knowledge played a crucial role in their own financial success and I was motivated to preserve this history for the younger generation.

CHAPTER 1

It is my hope that readers of this book will gain a different perspective on what it takes to be wealthy, and what it means to be wealthy. This is not a how-to book in the traditional sense. Making millions, for these entrepreneurs, is a task that takes the greater portion of a lifetime. It requires effort, sacrifice, risk-taking, and perseverance. Because of the presence of these mega-millionaires, Omaha is and will continue to be a vibrant, thriving community

CHAPTER 2: WHAT IS A MILLIONAIRE?

American culture has created an elaborate mythology around what is means to be rich. It is our tendency to believe that all wealthy individuals are immediately recognizable as such. We automatically connect "millionaire" status with certain occupations, geographical locations, and various external symbols of wealth such as fancy cars, expensive houses, and designer clothes. But let us take a closer, more practical look at what a millionaire is. A million dollars is, quite simply, 1,000,000 one-dollar bills, or 100,000 ten-dollar bills, or 10,000 one hundred dollar bills. That much is clear. But more important than what a million dollars is, is what a million dollars does. A million dollars buys $1,000,000 worth of goods or services. But what constitutes a million dollars worth of goods and services varies greatly over time. For example, in 1960, a million dollars would buy you a million dollars worth of 1960's goods. But if you had that 1960's million today, it would only buy you approximately $180,000 worth of goods. Conversely, if you could spend a million 1998 dollars in the year 1960, it would have been worth close to five million dollars in today's money. So, in terms of inflation, being a millionaire today isn't what it used to be. All things considered, it still isn't bad.

What, then, does it mean to be rich? At its most literal, a millionaire is one who has a million dollars free and clear. But more commonly, the term is used to denote an individual who is considered rich. But being rich is also a relative concept. When my son was young we were passing through a neighborhood of very large homes. We passed one home that was exceptionally ornate. Parked in the driveway was an old, beat-up car. My son asked, "If they are rich enough to live in a house like that, why do they have a car like that?" I responded, "Because they live in a house like that."

It is important to make the distinction between those who are financially successful and those who are materially successful. Society has the tendency to lump the two together and call the entire group rich. According to Webster's dictionary, rich means, "possessing much property and material goods." According to this definition, an individual with credit cards and long lines of credit meets the criteria for being rich. But, while society may classify an individual with significant amounts of unpaid-for goods as rich, such an individual does not necessarily meet the criteria for the financially successful.

To make the distinction between rich and financially successful we must first segregate the "rich" into the *affluent* and the *wealthy*. *Affluent* comes from the Latin word "afflue," which means to flow freely. *Wealth*, on the other hand, comes from the Anglo Saxon word "wela" which is defined as a great abundance of money and property. Thus, many of the rich are affluent. One could say that money flows through them like water through a sieve. They must work constantly in order to maintain the lifestyles they have created. The maximum richness they can attain is the sum of their income and credit card limits. Those individuals who are financially successful are wealthy in the true sense. They have both financial assets and material possessions. Their money works for them, and their lifestyles do not depend on the immediate fruits of their labor. Their ability to create wealth far exceeds their income and their credit limit. In the field of business, truly successful individuals are wealthy, not rich.

It is my observation, based on research, that, as a nation, Americans devote a considerable amount of time and effort toward the appearance of affluence, rather than toward the creation of wealth. In order to truly comprehend the nature of the wealthy, it is necessary to overcome the stereotypical images put forth by American culture. The images represented by the mass media are elementary ones, fixed on external symbols of wealth. If you were to take a close look at any city, including Omaha, you would find many individuals who appear to be millionaires. In some cases, you might be right. But in the majority of cases, you wouldn't be close. There are a significant number of individuals who I might classify as *millionaire decoys*. They look like a duck and quack like a duck, but they cannot fly.

To the experienced eye, the millionaire decoy is easy to spot. The decoy millionaire lives in a large, extravagant home and drives an expensive, imported car. Some of them live in "see-through" houses.

They were able to finance the house and the car, but ran out of money or credit or both before they got to the curtains and furniture. They may wear designer clothes and send their children to private schools. Finally, and perhaps most tellingly, they have the biggest and best grown-up "toys" such as cars, boats, electronic equipment, and vacation homes. They generally have jobs and titles that are consistent with this lifestyle, and some of these jobs often have appropriate salaries to go with them. However, they are only as solvent as their last paycheck, their savings, and whatever assets they could liquidate if need be. The important distinction here is that, while these individuals may be affluent, they are not necessarily wealthy.

In the effort to make the distinction between rich and wealthy, we invariably run into a particular problem. We have been conditioned to view money in a very narrow way. Specifically, we tend to believe that the financial upper crust is comprised solely of individuals who have large incomes. It is of vital importance to note that many individuals who are considered wealthy are not wealthy via their incomes. They are wealthy in a very different sense. That is to say, they acquired and grew valuable assets.

In order to gain a better understanding of the distinction between true millionaires and millionaire decoys, we'll employ some simple accounting tools: an income statement and a balance sheet. You do not have to be an accountant to utilize these aids. The arithmetic is patently clear and speaks for itself. Not only will these illustrations clarify the distinctions mentioned above, but they will assist in your understanding of how a great company operates, which will be discussed later.

Let us begin with an income statement. Put simply, it illustrates where money comes from and where it goes. The following represents an income statement of a typical millionaire decoy.

INCOME – OUT GO
Statement for typical millionaire decoy

Income		Expenses	
Salary	$250,000	Savings	$ - 0 -
Bonus	$100,000	Housing	$125,000
		Clothes	$ 48,000
		Food	$ 43,000
		Travel	$ 61,000
		Cars	$ 78,000
		Credit Card Interest	$ 38,000
Total Income	**$350,000**	**Total Expenses**	**$393,000**

CHAPTER 2

MAKING MILLIONS…INSTRUCTIONS INCLUDED

Based on appearances, these individuals are rich. The numbers, however, reveal a different scenario. The expenses of the millionaire decoy exceed his/her income. This analysis is not difficult but nonetheless illustrates a point about the rich that is so frequently overlooked; not everyone who appears to be wealthy is, in fact, wealthy. This is not to say that everyone who lives in an extravagant house or drives a fancy car is a millionaire-decoy. My point is that the appearance of wealth and actual wealth are not to be confused. To further illustrate this distinction, let's turn to the balance sheet for our decoy-millionaire. The concept of the balance sheet is quite simple. The balance sheet is comprised of two simple components: the value of one's assets and the value of one's liabilities. One figures the total value of liabilities and then subtracts that from the total value of assets. The remaining figure represents an individual's net worth.

ASSETS & LIABILITIES
Balance sheet for typical Omaha millionaire decoy

Assets		Liabilities	
House	$ 800,000	Mortgage	$ 710,000
Cars	$ 82,000	Student Loans	$ 52,000
Savings	$ 4,500	Bank Loan	$ 91,000
Toys (cars, boats, etc)	$ 76,000	Credit Cards	$ 67,000
Household Goods	$ 53,000	Saks Fifth Ave.	$ 37,000
		Loan From Parents	$ 57,000
Total Assets	**$1,015,500**	**Total Liabilities**	**$1,014,000**

On the surface, these individuals appear to be millionaires. They have large homes, expensive cars, several "toys," and typically, two professional careers. They have a million dollars worth of material possessions. They also have a million dollars worth of debt. Out of all the material possessions, only $1,500 of it actually belongs to them. The bottom line is that such an individual has a net worth of only fifteen hundred dollars.

Let's turn our focus now to an individual of real wealth. This individual's income statement looks considerably different from that of the millionaire decoy. One of the most noteworthy distinctions is that many genuine millionaires do not have a lot of income. Some studies have indicated that the real millionaire tends to be quite frugal when it comes to aspects of their personal lifestyles. They don't wear designer clothes, they tend to drive older, American-made cars, and, in general, they simply don't spend that much money. The implication here is that millionaires have more money because they save it. The reality is that these millionaires are not necessarily frugal by nature. Rather, the source of their wealth does not provide them with a large income. The following is an income statement that is not unusual for an individual of substantial wealth.

INCOME – OUT GO
Income Statement for a real Omaha millionaire

Income		Expenses	
Salary	$85,000	Housing	$ 38,000
Dividends	$36,000	Clothes	$ 9,000
Capital Gains	$58,000	Food	$ 21,000
		Cars	$ 8,000
		Travel	$ 2,100
		Savings	$100,900
Total Income	**$179,000**	**Total Expenses**	**$179,000**

The outgo of such individuals is actually less than their income, which is further reflected by their balance sheets. While the following balance sheet is hypothetical, it bears a close resemblance to the balance sheets of many wealthy individuals.

ASSETS & LIABILITIES
Balance sheet for typical Omaha millionaire

Assets		Liabilities	
Common Stock	$3,754,000	Mortgage	$ 21,784
House	$ 120,000	Dillard's	$ 984
Cars	$ 21,000	Taxes	$ 8,152
Household Goods	$ 18,500		
Savings	$ 47,623		
Total Assets	**$3,961,123**	**Total Liabilities**	**$ 30,920**

Total Assests – Total Liabilities = Net Worth $3,930,203

That's what a financially successful individual looks like. They don't necessarily have big incomes. They don't live extravagant lifestyles. But what they do have is a significantly large net worth.

It can be said that an entrepreneur is one who endeavors to create, own, and operate a business with the end goal of reaping its profits.

CHAPTER 2

Henry Ford, with his innovations in automobile technology and mass production is often cited as the archetypal entrepreneur. However, many successful entrepreneurs classify what they do by the type of ownership they have in their business. By owning the business as well as operating it, they take the risks and reap the rewards of success, or, they suffer the losses of failure. Nowadays, when we consider the term entrepreneur, it calls to mind these latter, owner-operators, whether they operate on a small or large scale.

Now let's turn our attention to Omaha's wealthy. There are approximately 120 people living in Omaha who have a net worth in excess of $100 million. When you consider that Omaha is a town of approximately 600,000 people, this is a significant number. The majority of these individuals are in the $400 to $500 million range. According to national statistics, there is one person worth $100 million for every 35,956 people in the United States. In Omaha, however, there is one person worth $100 million or more for every 4,932 people. My research has revealed that more than 10 people in Omaha qualify for the *Forbes'* "America's 400 Richest People" list. Only two are listed. In order to qualify for the 2000 *Forbes'* list, you have to have a net worth somewhere in excess of $500 million. Suffice it to say, these individuals are not your average millionaire next door.

It is difficult to find a word that is most representative of the wealth of these particular individuals. Originally, I referred to them as the "Omaha Millionaires." When I was young, I believed that millionaires were very special and rare. Today, however, achieving millionaire status is far more common than it used to be. So I moved on to the phrase "multi-millionaires." After all, these folks do have more than one million dollars, but so do the many Omahans who have $20 million. The individuals to whom I will be introducing you have much more than $20 million. In fact, a number of them are billionaires, or close to it. These individuals are not mere millionaires. They are *mega-millionaires*.

Furthermore, how do we truly comprehend what a billion dollars actually means? It is hard for us to imagine it in anything other than abstract terms. We know that a billion is a thousand million, and we can look at the zeros. But suppose you had a billion dollars in cash and you went on a shopping spree. Not in your lifetime could you buy enough cars, houses, clothes, or anything to equal a billion dollars. To illustrate the point, I looked at the Omaha real estate listings one day. On the day I checked there were fewer than $100 million worth of houses for sale in Omaha. So, for $100 million, you could have bought every house for sale in Omaha. Then what?

For the purpose of this book, I have created a few categories for Omaha's wealthy. Let's begin with Omaha's super-rich. I define the super-rich as those whose net worth is in excess of $100 million. In this group there are perhaps five or six individuals with a net worth of a billion dollars or more. Warren Buffett, chairman of Berkshire Hathaway, and Walter Scott, former head of Peter Kiewit Sons', Inc. both belong to this category. Buffett affiliates present a major challenge in determining net worth because their holdings are a closely guarded secret. But, when you get estimates in the $900 million range, we know they are either billionaires or close to it.

This group of super-rich can be divided in three subgroups. The first subgroup contains the patriarchs and matriarchs of Omaha's financial elite – I call them the "Old Guard". Most of these individuals have strong familial ties to Omaha, some going back to the turn of the century and before. Common to their success are a group of companies ranging from 52 years old to 144 years old. These companies have put Omaha on the map.

The majority of these companies were started by the Omaha mega-millionaires themselves. These include an insurance conglomerate, an agricultural implement manufacturer, an engineering firm, and the nation's largest retail furniture store. Others are second and third generation owners whose companies represent an eclectic mix. They include Omaha's largest bank, a store fixture manufacturer, and America's second largest-selling jewelry store next to Tiffany's in New York. The people in the Old Guard are mainly in their 70's and 80's now.

The next sub-group of the Omaha financial elite consists of second-generation owners who are mainly in their 50's. Their families are primarily from the middle socio-economic group, with a smattering of professionals thrown in. A number of their fathers were either engineers or store owners. None of these individuals came from families of significant financial means; however, all of the individuals in these two groups are self-made mega-millionaires. How can that be if I just told you that some of them inherited businesses? The businesses they inherited were adequate businesses with modest holdings, but the current generation took them, developed them, and turned them into tremendously successful mega-million dollar enterprises.

A third subgroup of super-rich are those who associated with Warren Buffett in what was to become Berkshire Hathaway. These are the Buffett Millionaires. Much has been written about Buffett's money and investment prowess but little of a public nature has been put forth about his partners. A strong factor in their obscurity lies in their desire to remain private.

And then there is the group I call the "New Guard." This group of super-rich is approximately one generation younger than the Old

Guard and the Buffett Partners. The companies they own and operate are also newer than those of the Old Guard. The family backgrounds are similar to those of the others in that they, too, are self-made, first generation millionaires. But since many of the companies they own are only ten to fifteen years old, their businesses have had less time to mature. About half of the companies included in this group have gone into areas that are electronic in nature such as telemarketing, telecommunications, and electronic brokerage.

It is important to understand that these are **not** "high-tech" companies, per se. High-tech companies are on the leading edge of innovation and development of sophisticated electronics and communications. In order to survive in that environment, a company must constantly spend capital on the development of new products. They must not only spend money but their efforts must constantly be successful. The Omaha companies in this group are end-users, not developers of these sophisticated products.

The New Guard individuals are mostly 40 to 50 year old entrepreneurs. Most of their businesses are quite young, having started in the 1980s and even early 1990s. Many are in service areas, such as telemarketing, banking and retail – with a significant member in fast food. Because this group is younger than the Old Guard, it will be interesting to see how this group develops as their businesses mature.

Making Millions seeks to investigate the phenomenon of Omaha's small group of extremely successful entrepreneurs. Its wealthiest residents have experienced a measure of success that exceeds the wildest dreams of the most dedicated small business owner. *Making Millions* attempts to address the question of why these individuals were successful and how they managed to do it.

These individuals have several key factors in common: the ownership of thriving companies, their midwestern location, and their undeniable success. The companies themselves offer a wide range of goods and services from construction to fast food. Despite this wide variety, these entrepreneurs have a great deal in common. Each of them exhibits a single-minded devotion to making their companies grow. They are willing to take the long view and pursue their company's growth over a period of years, reinvesting profits, and taking very little for themselves. In the following chapter, we will examine the creation of a successful company. This will provide for us greater insight into how these individuals achieved their great success.

CHAPTER 3: HOW A COMPANY MAKES ASSETS GROW

I have studied Omaha's mega-millionaires in great detail. And though they represent a wide variety of interests, they all share a common secret – the secret of wealth. One might expect this secret to be grand and guarded but, in actuality, it is quite simple. It boils down to this: the very wealthy own a significant interest in highly successful companies. The wealth of these individuals is due solely to their significant roles in these companies, not their occupations or the types of companies in which they are involved. In fact, the products and services that these companies provide are actually quite simple, which may come as a surprise to folks who believe that wealth through companies requires the invention of some exotic product or rare service. To put it simply, the wealthy did not attain their wealth from something or someone else. Rather, they created it through companies they founded (in most cases) and own.

At this point, some background discussion on the creation of wealth would be helpful. This chapter will be a bit more abstract in that I will ask you to look at some examples that will serve to illustrate a point. They are not necessarily real-world portraits of specific companies. This chapter will demonstrate for you how wealth is created and will show you how a company with a single, simple product can become a great company.

I feel a bit like Indiana Jones here as he is about to lay his hands on the Holy Grail because I have found out who the wealthy are and have some insight into how they got that way. What is most fun for me is telling you how the process works. For some of you, this rather basic economics lesson is familiar ground, but I think most readers will find the information worthwhile.

In a historical context, this method of becoming rich represents a relatively new phenomenon. Rich people have always existed, but the nature of the wealth has shifted dramatically over the years. The following explanation is a vast over-simplification, but it serves to illustrate a point. In earlier times, the wealthy were often rulers who controlled and exploited their natural resources or built an army, marched next door and took away the neighbors' gold. Economists and mathematicians call this a zero sum game. There is a finite amount of riches in one geographic area. If King A takes 1,000 pieces of gold from King B, King A is 1,000 pieces richer; King B is 1,000 pieces poorer. 1,000 plus added to 1,000 minus equals zero.

Eventually, over time, a second means of attaining wealth appeared. When money as we know it came into existence, there also came the custom of selling one's labor for cash wages. An individual could take the fruits of his or her labor and hoard them away to be spent at some future date. This, too, is close to a zero sum game. A boss pays for labor, thereby reducing the amount of money in his pocket and increasing the amount of money in the laborers' pockets by an equal amount. (What is not mentioned here is the value created by the laborer's efforts.) From the laborer's point of view, this is an asset accumulation process, similar to that of the king taking his neighbor's gold.

With the advent of capitalism, a further change occurred. Companies came into being and with them the possibility of asset growth. Let's begin with a few significant definitions. *Wealth accumulation* implies that there is a stream of money - mainly income from a job – and we gather it (save it) until there is a notable amount of money. *Asset growth*, on the other hand, is where we have an asset (the term economists use is capital). This can be a production plant, an idea, or a skill. By placing this asset into the economy, the actual value of it grows. You don't have to keep adding to it, it just gets bigger all by itself. However, in all my experience, the only thing that can actually make financial assets grow in value is a company.

In addressing this point I want to emphasize what growing assets is not. The perception of many people is that the very wealthy got that way because they are corporate executives, major-league athletes, or movie stars, and so they receive large, well-publicized incomes. Because of this, people assume that wealth is related to income.

Suppose that you are a highly paid professional such as a doctor or a lawyer. Your ability to make your net worth grow is entirely dependent upon your ability to perform your job. This is qualitatively different from owning a company, no matter how thoroughly you are trained and how highly you are compensated for your skills. Regardless of what you are paid per hour, and it may be several hundred dollars an hour, or even a thousand dollars an hour, your income level still has a finite cap. As long as your income depends on what you do for a living, you can only work so many hours in a day. Assuming that under an emergency situation the doctor or lawyer put in a 24 hour shift at $1,000 per hour. That is still a cap of $24,000 in one day. That is a lot of money, but (a) he or she cannot keep up that pace, and (b) he or she could never earn more than that at that rate. The point being, no matter how high your income rate, it still has a limit, not to mention the large portion that goes to the government.

Let's imagine this workaholic professional putting in a sixteen-hour day for one year, seven days a week, no holidays, at the rate of $1,000 per hour. He or she will, at the end of 365 days, have earned $5,840,000 gross income before taxes. This is a lot of money, but it will not put this workaholic in the ranks of the mega-millionaires we have discussed so far. At this pace, our exemplar of hard work will probably drop dead in a few years and still will not necessarily be a mega-millionaire. Most of our model mega-millionaires are alive and well and many of them live long lives, such as "Mrs. B" – Rose Blumkin. They work hard, but more importantly, they work smart.

In sum, while being highly paid and working long hours will earn you a healthy income, if not a healthy life-style, it is not the secret of *creating* wealth. In order for you to increase your net worth based on income, you need to continue to work, as pointed out above. If you are a famous actor and can ask for and receive $10 million per movie, you will have to be able to maintain that earning capacity in order to maintain or increase that level of wealth. Some actors can do that; many more cannot. Consider the following example. If you are 100% owner of a company, you will see how your net worth grows over time as the company grows. And you don't even have to be there all the time! In order for that company to develop and grow you would not be relying solely upon your own efforts. If you are prudent and follow the same path as the Omaha mega-millionaires, you will be hiring personnel to perform the essential functions of the company: producing the product, marketing it, delivering it, accounting for the costs and profits, and so on. It is a strong likelihood that in such a situation you are not going to have to work 24 hours a day or even 16 hours a day, though at times you might be there more than eight hours a day to supervise operations, plan future growth, deal with problems and so forth – all the normal ups and downs of working life, except you will be growing assets – not just earning wages – while you do it.

If you own a company, the growth of your net worth is not dependent upon or limited by the number of hours in a day. In fact, a common trait of the Omaha mega-millionaires and probably of successful business owners in general, is their ability to select the right people to do what needs to be done, to delegate those jobs and reward those people appropriately, thereby freeing themselves from continual direct involvement in the day-to-day operation of the company. If Bob Daugherty, for example, said that he and his two sons would produce all the center pivot irrigators for his company themselves, Valmont would never have grown to its present size and we would not be discussing Bob's success in this book.

As an aside, let's look briefly at *The Millionaire Next Door*, a book published not so long ago that describes a number of people who are worth over a million dollars but who are very obtrusive about it. The authors of that book sought to identify the traits these millionaires had in common that may have contributed to their accumulation of wealth. (Remember, these millionaires have a net worth of one to several million dollars but they are not the mega-millionaires described in this book.) That book notes that these millionaires are frugal, business owners, and so forth, in some ways similar to our Omaha group. But there is a significant difference. One of the things that separates the Omaha mega-millionaires from this group of business owners and "ordinary" millionaires is that many of these small business owners are just that – small business owners. They tend to remain very much involved in the day-to-day operation of their business as opposed to hiring other people to manage those functions and expand accordingly. Perhaps this is what makes them happy, but it is a subtle but very important distinction, one that may mean the difference between a stable-but-stagnant business and one that grows at an exponential rate, with profits to match.

For example, in the fast food industry, most of those who own such businesses hire managers to operate the shops. But ordinary millionaires have a tendency to remain involved in managing the managers while the mega-millionaire will hire managers to supervise the managers. The mega-millionaires will take a broader view and let other capable employees run the business. They are visionaries who can see how the business can grow and will direct its expansion into new markets. They are good organizers, efficient managers, and growth-centered. Once they reach a certain level of success they don't stop. Rather, they can see the big picture and let others handle the day-to-day concerns while they look at issues affecting future growth and guide the company or companies accordingly. These business owners may start out at the same place as ordinary millionaires, but they don't stop there.

Mega-millionaires are interested in challenges, adventures, and the next new thing. In a number of cases I have noted where a mega-millionaire would start an operation within the business, such as a new division, or a new product line. At first their excitement about the new area is tremendous and they are deeply involved with getting it established. But once it is established, functioning and running smoothly on its own, they are likely to turn it over to a subordinate to manage and they are then eager to move on to the next new challenge.

This trait of the mega-millionaires, creative delegation, reminds me of a scene from *Jeremiah Johnson*, a movie released in 1972 and starring Robert Redford as a man who goes to live in the mountains sometime in the last century. He is befriended by another mountain man by the name of Bear Claw (played by Will Geer). At one point in the movie, Jeremiah Johnson and Bear Claw are being chased by a bear. As they are running, Jeremiah asks Bear Claw, "Can you skin a griz?" "Yeah," says Bear Claw. So they keep running until they get to a cabin. Bear Claw runs into the cabin followed by the grizzly. Jeremiah slams the door after him and says, "Skin that one and I'll go get another one!" I will not attest to the accuracy of my memory, but you get the general idea. Mega-millionaires know how, when, and to whom to delegate, and this distinguishes them from ordinary millionaires.

The mega-millionaires attained their wealth through the process of **asset growth**. This is especially true in Omaha. It is difficult to grasp this concept without actual numbers, so I'll present the following example. In 1948, a young man from around Omaha had come back from World War II and was seeking to find his life's work. His total savings came to $5,000, which, at that time, was a considerable sum of money. He learned of an opportunity and with the $5,000 he purchased a small company that manufactured various pieces of light agricultural equipment. Over time this young man worked hard in his new company and prospered. New ideas came to him and the company grew. After a number of years he recognized his need to obtain additional capital in order for his company to experience its real potential – to expand and develop in keeping with his vision for the company. He issued stock, shares of ownership in the company, and thus became a partner in the business with many others.

Fast forward to today. This man still owns stock in his own company, along with many other people. His net worth from his ownership of the stock in the company is around *two hundred and twenty million dollars* – $220,000,000. This illustrates how $5,000, plus a great deal of hard work, can become, over the years, $220,000,000.

This is *asset growth*. If he had begun with his savings of $5,000 and just accumulated it, i.e. – saved it for 50 years, he would have a fair amount of money. It would not, however, come close to his present number of $220,000,000. Let's go one step further: let's assume he had a $5,000 a year income that he saved and put in the bank for 50 years. His net worth after 50 years would be $314,092.75, after taxes. Again, this is not close, so let's bump him up ten times to a $50,000 a year job and assume the same scenario. His net worth today would be $3,140,927.50. This figure would send him into the ranks of the ordinary millionaires but he is still a long, long way from $220,000,000. That's the difference between wealth accumulation and asset growth. By means of *asset growth*, rather than just saving, or wealth accumulation, not only does our enterprising man now have $220,000,000 worth of stock, he also has the income from his job as president of the company and all the dividends the company has paid over the years.

Now the crucial question: HOW DOES A COMPANY MAKE MONEY GROW IN VALUE? The only economic unit that can consistently, in an understandable and predictable fashion, grow the value of money is a company. If you can understand the process by which companies increase the value of money, you will be able to understand how the Omaha millionaires and others like them got to be that way.

The Omaha companies are great companies, exceptional in many ways. But it is important to define what makes a good or great company. I don't claim to provide a definitive answer, and there are many different ways to measure the success of a company. However, one of the measures we might look at here is the company's overall size: the scope of its operations, how many employees, etc. I believe it is ABC which says, "More people get their news from ABC than from any other source in the world." This may or may not reflect ABC's actual success, but it is one yardstick that may be used. Another way that companies are often evaluated is in the amount of the market share they have cornered in their given area. This is a fairly common measure that many companies, such as car manufacturers for example, use to measure their success. A third yardstick that applies to technologically oriented companies, such as computer software or hardware companies, for example, is the question of whether they have produced any new developments this year. Are we creating more and different types of software or hardware than our competitors? Are we leaders in innovations in our field?

For the purposes of examining the Omaha mega-millionaire companies, I believe that the best way to measure success is to evaluate the amount of financial return they get based upon the amount of capital they have put into the business. This is basically asking the question, "what is the return on your investment?" Companies may brag about being a billion-dollar company, but if they put in $950 million and saw a return of only $50 additional million, that is not a large return. So I am looking at rate of return in comparison to the original investment.

The three measurements I mentioned earlier – overall size, market share, and leadership in the field – hearken back to the personality or ego and values of the CEO and what he or she wants to be recognized for. The fourth measurement I mentioned, "what is the rate of return on my investment," typifies the approach of some of the Omaha mega-millionaires. What is important to them is not necessarily their size, market share, or leadership in the field, though all of these things may play a role from time to time. Rather, they look at how well the company is doing and how well they are playing the game of growing their company. Success for a successful company is not only about money – they have that many times over – it is about the challenge of the game of business itself.

Let's look at an imaginary company so we can see, in practical terms, how this process works. When I was an economics professor, my colleagues and I always used examples such as "Widget Company." I never knew what a widget was. They don't sound very appealing. So let's use something a little more interesting. Nebraska is "The Cornhusker State" known for its corn and college football. So our example is going to be "Cloyd & Clyde's Colossal Corn Chip Company."

The Cloyd and Clyde Colossal Corn Chip Company is the brainchild of two cousins from Crete, Nebraska, Cloyd and Clyde Clapper. Because corn is so readily available in Nebraska, as it is throughout the Midwest, the Clapper cousins grew up with corn as a constant part of their environment. But they got the idea for their corn chips from their cousin Carrie from Cleveland. While visiting Carrie they accidentally knocked some cayenne pepper into a bowl of corn chips sitting on the counter. They took a bite and said, "Wow! This is great!" And so out of a simple idea came the "Colossal Corn Chips with Clout." (The actual amount of cayenne pepper and other spices added to the chips is a recipe that remains a closely guarded company secret to this day.)

How did the company start? We take two people with some money to invest and a little of the entrepreneurial spirit (which means they are willing to take a few risks). Both Cloyd and Clyde invested $500 in the company. They each have 500 shares at $1 a share. The company has $1,000 in cash, no debt at this point, and therefore a net worth of $1,000. They are starting small, but watch.

With its cash, the company secures the raw materials and machinery needed to produce its corn chips. At the end of the **first year**, the company's books look like this:

EXPENSES	
Mixing bowls, frying equipment and a crude factory	$333.33
Cornmeal and frying oil	$333.33
Labor and distribution	$333.33
Total Spent	**$1,000.00**

INCOME	
Number of bags of chips produced	400
Actual cost per bag	$2.50
Sales price per bag	$3.00
Total Income	**$1,200.00**

At the end of the first year, the company has made a profit of $200. But it has a net worth of $1,533 (a 50% increase) if you consider the possibility of selling off the bowls and equipment at cost.

At the start of the second year, the company already has the necessary means of production. Because they already own the means of production, the company begins its second year with $1,200 in cash. They don't need to repeat their *startup costs*. They can spend the entire $1,200 on raw materials and produce more chips than before.

So the books for the end of the second year look like this:

EXPENSES	
Mixing bowls, frying equipment	$0
Cornmeal and frying oil	$600.00
Labor and distribution	$600.00
Total Spent	**$1,200.00**

The owners then funneled the proceeds back into the company, and increased production. Their income looks like this:

INCOME	
Number of bags of chips produced	700
Actual cost per bag	$1.71
Sales price per bag	$3.00
Total Income	**$2,100.00**

Note that several things have happened here. The cost of producing a bag of Cloyd and Clyde's Corn Chips has declined by 79 cents or 31%. This is because the physical means of production are paid for, but the price consumers were willing to pay for the product remained constant. Thus, profits increased and the company is now worth $2,433 (cash plus the value of the physical assets). You can argue and I think reasonably that the value of the equipment has depreciated, or declined over the passage of time. This may be true if they want to sell their used equipment. But it still provides the same production power to the company, so for the purposes of this discussion we will ignore depreciation.

Now we enter the third year and life at Cloyd and Clyde's company is good. First of all, they want to dramatically increase their production, so they need to invest more money in plants and equipment. Several things happen. First, because the new equipment makes the production line more efficient, labor costs don't go up appreciably. Second, because they are buying larger quantities of raw materials, the per-unit price of the raw materials actually declines. And further, the chips have been around long enough now for people to notice that Cloyd and Clyde's Chips do taste different, and perhaps they are willing to pay a little bit more to munch on such a special, hot and spicy chip that really is much better than your ordinary chip.

Now, the third year income statement looks like this:

EXPENSES	
Mixing bowls, frying equip., etc.	$600.00
Cornmeal and frying oil	$900.00
Labor and distribution	$600.00
Total Spent	**$2,100.00**

CHAPTER 3

INCOME	
Number of bags of chips produced	1700
Actual cost per bag	$1.23
Sales price per bag	$3.33
Total Income	**$5,661.00**

    At the end of the third year, the company has a net worth of $6,327 and an initial investment of $1,000. Do you think that $3.33 is a bit of a stretch to pay for the bag of snack chips used in this example? Corn and potatoes are cheap. But have you bought a bag of potato chips, a box of snack crackers, or a box of cereal lately? I bet you have, and if so, have you thought about how much it actually costs to make those chips, snacks, or cereal? You can make your own potato or corn chips and they are delicious, albeit time consuming and messy. Most of us don't do that. We pay the $1.99, $2.99, or more for our snacks and cereal made with commercial equipment by someone else, rather than spend our own time, energy, and cooking oil to make them at home.

    Admittedly, this is a simplified version of the production process and things don't always go as smoothly in the real world as they did for Cloyd and Clyde and their Colossal Corn Chip Company. But my hope is that it helps to illustrate the concept of establishing a profitable company. People do it all the time, and what is important to remember is that a company does not have to do extraordinary things to get extraordinary results. The Omaha mega-millionaires prove this. What it requires is the discipline to properly run the company.

    In order for a company producing seemingly ordinary products to achieve these types of results it must:
1. Make certain that it controls the relationship between its costs and the selling price of its product.
2. Make sure that the consumer sees their products as better or at least different and therefore more desirable than those of the competition.

    At the center of this issue is a concept that I will call, for lack of a better term, "Brand Name Phenomenon." People perceive some brands as better or different than others, for which, as far as anyone can tell, there is no intrinsic reason. Some people insist on "Coke," or "Pepsi" when they buy a soft drink. Others are willing to pay extra for a shirt with a "Tommy Hilfiger" or "Ralph Lauren" designer label, when it is essentially no different than any shirt, made anywhere, without a little logo.

One summer my wife bought our son a golf shirt similar to those worn by his friends. On the upper left front it had an embroidered horseman about one half of an inch high. The horseman carried a flag and the shirt sold at Richman Gordman (a Midwestern Discount store) for about $23. My son worked that summer and before returning to school in the fall, he returned the shirt in question to me for my use. He replaced it with a nearly identical shirt with only two differences: the embroidered horseman carried a polo mallet and the shirt cost $55!

I am reasonably certain that these two very similar shirts cost approximately the same to produce. But my son's perception and that of his friends is that the name brand shirt is preferable to any other shirt of that type, and they will pay what they can for the brand. At the risk of understatement, I think I can say that this phenomenon has been noticed by parents with great frequency in recent years.

In order to explore these ideas a little further, let's compare our corn chip company with one that produces a more technically complicated product. Please remember that these are hypothetical examples and are provided in simplified form to illustrate my point.

Cloyd and Clyde have two other cousins from Claymore, named Chris and Claire. Chris and Claire are impressed with the success of the corn chip company, but are not interested in producing anything so mundane as a corn chip. They decide to form a company to produce something more high-tech, computer chips. So Chris and Claire's Creative Computer Chip Company is born.

Just as Cloyd and Clyde did, Chris and Claire invest in their company. Both put up $5,000 to get the company started. They each get 500 shares worth $10 a share. The company has $10,000 in cash, no debt, and therefore a net worth of $10,000.

As was true for the corn chip company, the computer chip company buys with its cash the equipment and materials necessary to produce its creative computer chips. At the end of the first year, their books look like this:

EXPENSES	
Computer chip machines	$2,500
Raw materials	$2,000
Research and development	$4,500
Labor and distribution	$1,000
Total Spent	**$10,000**

CHAPTER 3

INCOME	
Number of chips produced	600
Actual cost per chip	$16.66
Sales price per chip	$18.33
Total Income	**$11,000.00**

Notice the difference here from the experience of the corn chip company. Cloyd and Clyde essentially stumbled across the design of their corn chip. But with computer chips, more is involved. Presumably computer chips require a significant amount of technical knowledge up front and will require a continued and ongoing effort on the part of their manufacturers if they are to stay abreast of technological changes and ahead of their competition. Also note that Chris and Claire started with ten times the capital of Cloyd and Clyde.

At the end of the first year, the Creative Computer Chip Company had a profit of $1,000 (five times as much as the profit realized by the Colossal Corn Chip Company in absolute terms, but then Chris and Claire also had to invest ten times as much to do that). If you make the same assumptions as we did about the Corn Chip Company, the Computer Chip Company has a net worth of $2,500, or an increase of 25% from their beginning.

Remember, this is a hypothetical example. But we can look at some typical developments here. At the start of the second year the company has $11,000 in capital and like the corn chip company, they now own the physical equipment necessary for production. As before, they have more capital to spend on raw materials and they can increase the number of units produced. But some significant differences remain. The corn chip company has been able to convince its consumers that it's because of the secret ingredients or special recipe that their product is different. In the computer chip market, a part is a part. The primary distinction between Creative Computer Chip Company and other companies is price. So in order to keep their customers, the Creative Chip Company must match their competitors' price. The struggle for survival is over the cost of production of the chips. Assuming that the quality of the product is similar to that of other products of the same type, the company that can produce the chips for the lowest price will be the most profitable.

There is a second wrinkle. In this environment, innovation and the development of smaller, faster, more versatile chips is important. This company is dependent upon technology. The Creative Computer Chip Company must create new innovations and new products at least as fast as its competitors. To the extent they can out-innovate the competition they will prosper. But innovation does not come without a price and that cost is ongoing.

So here is what their books look like at the end of the second year:

EXPENSES	
Computer chip machines	$0
Raw materials	$2,500
Research and development	$6,000
Labor and distribution	$2,500
Total Spent	**$11,000**

INCOME	
Number of chips produced	700
Actual cost per chip	$15.71
Sales price per chip	$18.00
Total Income	**$12,600**

As you can see, at the end of the second year the increase in outlay for research and development has paid off. The Creative Computer Chip Company has been able to decrease its cost of production and has been able to sell more units. But they were forced by competitive pressures to reduce the selling price of their product.

The third year of business presents many options in terms of the direction the company can take to achieve further success. My purpose here is not to argue that one type of company is better than the other, but to show how typical companies work and how their net worth increases over time. In our examples, one company produces a simple product involving little or no research and development, and another company produces a more technical product where innovation will play a role in how competitive they are. Both have the potential to do well. What is important here is to understand how companies produce their products and how a company can be quite successful at doing something relatively simple.

The bigger the difference between the cost of the production and the sale price, the faster the company grows. The faster the company grows, the faster the value of its financial assets grows. The company needs to convince the market that its product is somehow different from that of its competitors, or, as in the second example, that the product is more efficient or cheaper than that of the competitors, and they will succeed. The better they are able to accomplish this, the greater will be the profits. *But notice this!* a company doesn't have to do anything extraordinary in order to gain a significant return on its capital.

THE BOTTOM LINE: Companies can dramatically grow the value of financial assets by the way they develop their products. Furthermore, individuals who become truly successful are the ones who own such companies. To reinforce this one more time, let's compare the difference between putting $10,000 in a bank and $10,000 in a company. To help you see the difference it is necessary for you to understand what the term *margin* means. The *margin* is the difference between the cost of producing a product and the amount of money that the product can be sold for, in a sense, its profitability. This can be compared to an interest rate. You put dollars in a bank and the rate of return is the interest rate. In the case of a company, you put dollars into a business and the rate of return is called the margin.

But *margin* and *interest* are very different:

BANK	**COMPANY**
$10 Deposit	$10 Cost of producing a product
Value in one year: $10.50	Selling price of product: $13
Interest rate: 5%	Margin: 30%

Because of the structure of the American economy, it is possible for some companies to "grow" the purchasing power of a dollar in a fashion that no other entity can.

Let's assume that we have $10,000 and we wish to increase its value. These are our assumptions about Colossal Corn Chip Company:
- Margins of 35%
- Inflation is 3%
- Bank pays 5% interest (2% over inflation)
- Example is for one-year period.

Net change in purchasing power or value over the course of a year with the money invested in the company:

TYPE OF EXPENSE OF RETURN REALIZED	AMOUNT
Amount spent to create product (cost)	$10,000
Total revenue or income (sales)	$13,500
Net gain (sales minus cost)	$3,500
Inflation	$ 405
Net change in purchasing power	**$3,095**

Compare this with the same amount of money deposited with a bank:

AMOUNT DEPOSITED	$10,000
Total returned at maturity (one year for this example)	$10,500
Net gain	$ 500
Inflation	$ 315
Net change in purchasing power	**$ 185**

In the case of the bank deposit, the interest rate (margin) is always going to be a function of inflation, and therefore the real rate of growth of purchasing power will be in the range of 2%. A company can grow faster, have larger margins (interest rate) based on how successfully they sell their product.

This chapter shows how anyone, *anyone*, can start up a company with a relatively modest initial investment. It will generally cost more than the $500 or $5,000 mentioned here, but still, many people do start their own companies with only a small amount of capital in the beginning. Many of them are quite successful. What distinguishes the mega-millionaire from the ordinary millionaire is a question of degree – not type. The mega-millionaire becomes entranced by the gamesmanship of growing companies, and continues to do so. Success breeds success and contributes to the growth of multi-million-dollar companies. The best way to understand this is to take a look at some of Omaha's mega-millionaires. We will begin by looking at the common backgrounds of these individuals in order to see the foundation that formed their considerable success.

CHAPTER 4: STARTING FROM SCRATCH: COMMON CHARACTERISTICS OF OMAHA'S MEGA-MILLIONAIRES

During my years in Omaha and in the course of my research, I have had the opportunity to sit down face-to-face with many of Omaha's wealthiest individuals. It is a fascinating and humbling experience to encounter someone whose background and upbringing is similar to yours or mine, but whose assets amount to millions. Let us look at some of the characteristics that many of these individuals have in common.

Of particular interest and importance is the fact that none of Omaha's mega-millionaires were born into their wealth. Most come from what would best be described as a middle-class background. They were not impoverished, but they were not wealthy. It could be said that all Omaha money is new money, even that of the Old Guard. There are a handful of exceptions – situations where the son or relative of a business owner inherited a business and took it to unimagined levels of success. But an astonishing 98% of the wealth within this group was created by its members from scratch.

These individuals are the children of hardworking shopkeepers, schoolteachers, and farmers. The middle-class childhood of these mega-millionaires was exactly the same as that of most Omahans of their generation. Their family situations did not provide them with any significant economic or social privileges that would serve to launch them into astounding financial success. However, they all inherited something far more significant. They inherited a system of values and a work ethic that would provide for each of them a solid foundation for success.

The values held by the mega-millionaire families were those that dominated the urban and rural Midwest during the first half of the twentieth century. There existed at that time a widespread belief that one's success in life was directly correlated to one's own efforts, and hard work would result in the opportunity to provide oneself and one's family with a comfortable living. In addition, there were definite limits on how much one really needed in order to get by.

These values were particularly visible in the Midwest, where many individuals came from or were connected to farm communities. A farm community is keenly and constantly aware of its tenuous stability and on the basis of that awareness, tends to live one year at a time. Several of Omaha's wealthy actually lived on farms or had relatives who did. They learned firsthand that though one might be having a good year, the next year could likely bring floods or drought. Therefore, one never wasted money on frivolous items because that money might be needed for survival in the coming year. In these families, a pattern of living was established. Thus, merely achieving affluence one year was not reason enough to suddenly change one's level of consumption. If one were frugal, the rewards of good years would carry a family through trials of more difficult ones.

These rural values comprise a portion of the foundation that many of Omaha's wealthy individuals hold in common. Another aspect of this firm foundation is creativity and ingenuity in the face of challenging circumstances. For the individuals who lived through it, the Great Depression was a devastating time. Many view the stock market as a major factor in their economic plight and are therefore fearful of investments. However, I believe that the Omaha experience during the Depression differed somewhat from that of the rest of the country, even the rest of Nebraska. Rural Nebraska was hit very hard by the Depression because of the tremendous decline in the prices of farm commodities. In contrast, some of the Omaha companies that are now associated with mega-millionaires were either formed during the Great Depression, or prospered in the face of it. This is especially true of firms in the engineering and construction business. As the Depression deepened, the Federal Government funded many large construction jobs that would serve to provide employment opportunities and salaries. Several Omaha construction firms took advantage of this opportunity. In 1930's Nebraska, the Public Works Administration built 52 schools, 41 waterworks, 13 bridge projects, and 11 sewage disposal plants. The salaries provided by these jobs had a positive effect on the economy of Omaha, which, to a certain degree, softened the impact of the Depression. In addition to this positive growth, the money that engineers and construction workers were earning was being spent in Omaha, which in turn provided further income to everyone from grocers to sales clerks.

Several of Omaha's numerous construction and engineering firms owe some of their current success to the government activity designed to bring the Depression to an end. Firms such as HDR and Peter Kiewit Sons', Inc. experienced major business growth in the 1930's which continued through the war and the postwar eras.

In terms of investing, the Depression impacted everyone's attitude. The general public became very conservative with their finances and quite leery of the stock market. The response of the Omaha millionaires, however, was very different. They positioned themselves in such a way that they would never be in that condition again. Instead of basing their decisions on the fear of risk-taking, they decided to use their modest resources to promote further investment. They never lost sight of the necessity of risk-taking.

As we continue to examine the foundation that served our Omaha millionaires, it is important to look at the role of education. For the most part, this group's early education took place in public schools. For them, prep schools and tutors were for other people. Omaha has a longstanding reputation of quality public secondary education. There are many members of the Old Guard who graduated from Central High School, a large urban high school whose imposing building still sits on a hill on the northeast corner of Dodge Street near Omaha's downtown. Today, the population of Omaha has shifted approximately twenty miles to the west, but Central High School continues to enjoy the reputation of a quality school. It is staggering to consider the incredible amount of wealth that can be represented at a typical Central class reunion.

In terms of higher education, most of Omaha's mega-millionaires continued in public schools. The state colleges and universities attended by our group include the University of Nebraska at Lincoln, University of Nebraska at Omaha, Colorado State, Iowa State and the University of Omaha. As for business degrees, the only MBA's among the Old Guard belong to Warren Buffett and Mike Harper. Among the New Guard, the only MBA that I was able to identify belongs to Ken Stinson, the current head of Peter Kiewit Sons', Inc. The most common major among this group is engineering.

To the best of my knowledge, there are no earned Ph.D.'s in the group. There are, however a number of honorary ones. For example, Mrs. B, Vinod Gupta and Walter Scott have all received honorary degrees for their significant business success and for their notable support of the community in which they live.

Although Omaha's wealthy made their millions in a wide variety of ways, their backgrounds were quite similar. None of them were born into their level of wealth. Most of them came from middle class, hardworking families, and nearly all of them were educated at local, public schools. It is important to recognize that the wealth of these individuals did not come to them via inheritance or exceptional formal training in the field of business; many of them were trained in the field of engineering. Their success came from hard work, strong personal characteristics, vision, and foresight.

CHAPTER 5: THE PEOPLE
OF THE OMAHA FINANCIAL COMMUNITY

Just how unusual is the Omaha financial community? In the previous chapter, I showed by way of an overview that many of Omaha's wealthy have characteristics in common and come from backgrounds that are comparable to one another. Now it is time to look at this wealth in a way that removes it from the realm of the abstract.

Clearly, a great deal of wealth exists in Omaha. Several issues factor into this phenomenon but of particular interest is the interconnectivity of these individuals. They didn't accomplish their lofty achievements in a vacuum. The Omaha financial community is comprised of a whole network of synergetic relationships. Over time, the community developed a set of common values that greatly contributed to the success of it members. In this chapter, we will follow the success patterns of several model individuals who provided inspiration and support to this community.

Now it's time to meet some Omaha mega-millionaires whose lives and histories illustrate the principles of this book. These are people who founded or acquired ownership of companies. Their products are, for the most part, simple, non-technological goods which anyone can make or buy. They came from modest backgrounds. Some were college-educated; others had no education at all. But they all worked hard, made modest profits, and reinvested in their companies, making them grow. They did not squander their wealth. They did not conspicuously consume. But most importantly, and paradoxically, they did take risks, especially in the establishment and expansion of their companies. They were not afraid to strike out on their own. I have selected individuals from the previously described "Old Guard" and "New Guard" to serve as representative examples of the group as a whole. From their biographies, you will see the diversity of their backgrounds and activities. What will also emerge are the things they have in common which have helped make them who they are.

THE BLUMKIN FAMILY

One early member of the Old Guard was Rose Blumkin, popularly known as Mrs. B. Her discount furniture business grew from a very modest start to a multi-million dollar business over the course of her lifetime. She loved what she did and continued to work right up until the day of her death at 103.

Mrs. B, the founder of Nebraska Furniture Mart, was, for the 79 years she lived in Omaha, the local icon for hard work. "The Mart," as it is referred to by the locals, began in 1935, and today it is one of the largest single home furnishings complexes in the United States. The complex has more than one million square feet of sales floor situated on 75 acres of land. In 1993, the Mart expanded by adding an appliance and electronics division. It serves an area within a 300-mile radius of Omaha by selling everything from rugs to sofas, lamps to cell phones. All of this results in annual sales in excess of $300 million. How profitable are they? No one outside the Blumkin family and Warren Buffett know the answer to that. As is true with many discount stores, prices are very reasonable. Every item in the Mart is "marked down" but no outsider knows "marked down" from what? The store is clearly successful, but Mrs. B's story is in itself even more interesting.

Mrs. B was born in Russia on the eve of Hanukkah in 1893. One of eight children, her father was a rabbi and her mother ran a small grocery store. At 13, she managed to move to a larger city where she found employment in a dry goods store. At 16 she was managing the store and its six male employees.

In 1914, she met and married a shoe salesman named Isador Blumkin. Shortly thereafter, the start of World War I forced Isador to flee to the U.S. to avoid being drafted into the Russian army. Three years later, Mrs. B managed to make her way to the Chinese border, where a Russian guard stopped her. She told him she was on a trip to buy leather for the army and promised she would bring him a bottle of vodka on her return. He let her pass. She never returned. She managed to get to Japan and then by boat to Seattle.

She caught up with Isador in Fort Dodge, Iowa, and soon they moved to Omaha where a number of other Russians had gathered. Isador opened a second-hand clothing store at 1211 Dodge Street. His wife helped him when she could, while learning to speak English from their four children.

CHAPTER 5

In 1932, her parents, one brother, four sisters, and a cousin came to this country. Rose Blumkin began helping her husband in his second-hand store. Her knack for inventive merchandizing led to the printing of 10,000 circulars that offered to dress any man "From head to toe for $5." That included a suit of clothes, hat, shoes, shirt, tie, and underwear. In 1937, Mrs. B borrowed $500 from a relative and opened her own furniture store at 1312 Farnam Street, across the alley from her husband's business. Billionaire Warren Buffett once remarked, "Imagine what she could have done if she'd started with more?"

Warren Buffet and "Mrs. B."

On August 31, 1983, Warren Buffett approached Mrs. B and said, "Today is my birthday and I want to buy your store. How much do you want for it?" Mrs. B replied, "Sixty million dollars." Buffett went to get a check, returned and they settled on a price of $55 million for 80% of the store, with present management retaining a stake of 20%. A one-page contract closed the deal with Mrs. B making a mark – she could not read or write English. The transaction was completed without an audit of the Mart's books or inventory. No lawyers scrutinized the deal. This attitude of trust and decisive action is common among this group.

To her employees, the demanding Mrs. B could be a difficult boss. She had an up-and-down relationship with members of her own family, as shown by her angry departure from the Mart in 1989. She maintained that her grandsons, Ronald and Irvin Blumkin, then president and vice-president, respectively, had undermined her authority in the Mart's carpet department. Three months later, she opened a store in a brick warehouse that she owned just north of the Furniture Mart. Mrs. B ran the carpet department and leased the rest of the building to other home furnishings businesses.

As time passed, the differences between Mrs. B and the grandsons began to heal. Her warehouse was profitable, but she was pushing the century mark. During her later years, Mrs. B began receiving the recognition she deserved. In 1984, New York University awarded her an honorary Doctorate of Commercial Science. Creighton University awarded her an honorary Doctor of Laws degree, and she was inducted in the Nebraska Business Hall of Fame. On December 3, 1997, Mrs. B turned 103. During the early months of 1998 she continued to sell carpet at the Mart, but by summer her work schedule had become uncharacteristically inconsistent.

Mrs. B died on August 10th, 1998 at the age of 103. Only two days earlier she had worked at the Mart. The Mart remained open on the day of her funeral. Her grandson, Robert Batt, said, "She would have liked it that way." Mrs. B and others like her built their businesses through hard work. More importantly, they funneled back into the business the profits that they realized, rather than spending them on an affluent lifestyle. Their net worth grew not just to a million but to *millions.* Could the immigrant from Russia have ever predicted that her rather ordinary discount furniture and carpet business would one day be valued in the 10's of millions? Probably not.

THE BUFFETT PARTNERS

Say the words *Omaha* and *millionaire* and if the next words out of your mouth aren't "Warren Buffett," then you have been on some other planet for the past few decades. I am not going to re-tell the Buffett story here, because that has been told elsewhere. (You may wish to read one of Andrew Kilpatrick's books about Buffett.) But there is another interesting aspect to the Buffett story that has not been widely documented. It is the story of the many ordinary Omahans who were there with Buffett at the beginning and went along with him for the investment ride of their lives. Had these people not been willing to put up their own money and allow him to manage it, there would not be a Warren Buffett story. Buffett is another example of the successful entrepreneur who loves the business of business. He has repeatedly said that he would never retire, and that they will have to hold séances so people can benefit from his investment advice after he is gone.

In May of 1956, Warren Buffett began seeking investors who were willing and able to put money into the Buffett Partnership. He was 25 years old at the time and the initial investors consisted of four family members and three close friends. The original non-family members were Charles E. Peterson, Jr., Elizabeth B. Peterson (Charles' mother) and attorney Daniel J. Monen, Jr. Charles and Daniel invested $5,000 each, while Charles' mother contributed $35,000. (As a point of reference, Warren's initial investment was $100.)

As time passed more partners were added and some of the original partners continued to add money to the fund. In 1962, the Buffett partnership began buying shares of a financially depressed New England textile company named Berkshire Hathaway. Buffett continued to buy Berkshire shares throughout the 1960's and in 1970 he was made chairman of the board. This would become the core investment vehicle for the partnership. Other companies were added in the ensuing years. Some of the other individuals who came aboard included students of night investment classes that he taught at Omaha University (Now the University of Nebraska at Omaha). Investors learned about Buffett's activities through word of mouth. The fund began with $105,100 in cash. The agreement stated that Buffett held the responsibility for investing these dollars and making them grow. He was to invest the money without the advice or knowledge of the partners. He would then keep twenty-five percent of the profits when they exceeded a return of six percent. The business was wildly successful.

CHAPTER 5

Following the initial years, new dollars and new partners were added. This continued until the number of partners reached 99, at which point Buffett stopped taking new investors. The reason for this lies in the security regulations that require a significant increase in financial disclosure when a partnership exceeds 99. Buffett's preference was to operate with as little scrutiny as possible. By the time the magic partnership number was reached, the assets of the venture had grown to $17 million. Documents filed with the Douglas County Clerk reveal that 49 of the partners were residents of Omaha. While the number of partners is known, we are unable to establish the number of individuals involved, because by law "Partners" could either be individuals or groups of individuals.

One example of the group partner aspect is Dr. Carol Angle. In 1957, Dr. Angle, a young pediatrician, enrolled in an investment course at Omaha University taught by Buffett. Angle had heard that he was a bright kid and she wanted to hear what he had to say. She said, "Warren had us calculate how money would grow, using a slide rule." She was persuaded, and she and her husband, William, also a doctor, invited 11 other doctors to meet with Warren. At the meeting the Angles announced, "We're putting in $10,000. The rest of you should, too." Eventually, 10 doctors formed a group called Mdee, Ltd. which became a Buffett partner.

In 1970 Buffett decided to terminate the partnership and the partners who wished to continue would become Berkshire Hathaway shareholders. A number opted out and received either bonds or cash in exchange for their partnership shares.

Buffett offered the partners three options: They could take cash; he would help them place their assets in bonds; or they could take shares of Berkshire Hathaway, the poor-performing New England mill that constituted the bulk of the partnership assets. Some of the partners, such as Ethel Bjornsen and her late husband Olaf of Colome, South Dakota, chose cash. At that time, their $5,000 investment had grown to $50,000. In her words, "We were young and thought we could do better with it ourselves." The exact number who took the Berkshire stock is not known, but we do know what happened to those who did. Those who invested $5,000 are now worth about $200 million plus. Those who invested more are worth possibly as much as $1 billion. The point here is that investors like Buffett do not make their money simply by saving it – they purchase and own companies whose assets grow and thereby benefit the investors. I will be talking more about this later on.

In the summer of 1998, Jim Rasmussen, a reporter for the *Omaha World-Herald* made an effort to identify and interview the remaining

Buffett partners still living in Omaha. Ten of them spoke to him and the rest declined. There is positive identification of 10, but there's a possibility that the actual number might be a high as 25. While the interviews avoided specifics on their current holdings, they were open with stories about their early experiences with Buffett.

Most of this group lead quiet lives. Like the typical Omaha millionaires, they live in nondescript houses, drive regular cars and seldom eat at fancy restaurants nor spend their evenings at elegant cocktail parties. Most are in their late 60's and early 70's. Some have very close relatives who have no clue about the size and nature of their wealth. Most of them will spend an incredibly small portion of their Berkshire millions on themselves. Some will personally use none of it. It is impossible to tell how many kids or grandkids have gone through college or bought their first house with shares of Berkshire Hathaway. It is also impossible to tell how many wings have been added on to churches and hospitals because of Berkshire money.

Billionaire Neighborhood

CHAPTER 5

VINOD GUPTA

Vinod Gupta was born in the village of Rampur Manhyaran, located approximately 100 miles north of New Delhi. At the time of Gupta's birth, the village had no electricity, paved roads, televisions or cars. Gupta's arrival in the U.S. follows the classic story line – only $58 in his pocket and all his worldly possessions in one suitcase. Gupta entered the University of Nebraska and received his engineering degree in 1969. He spent another two years at the University of Nebraska Lincoln, earning a Masters degree in Business Administration in 1971.

Following his graduation, Gupta moved to Omaha, finding work as a marketing research analyst with Commodore Corporation, a manufacturer of mobile homes with 18 plants around the country. While at Commodore, Vinod was assigned the task of getting a list of every mobile home dealer in the United States. He bought lists from all the business list companies existing at the time, and found them to be incomplete and out of date. He felt he could do better, so he ordered all available 4,800 Yellow Pages phone directories and set out to compile the list himself!

When the books were delivered, they filled up the entire reception area; no one could get through the door of the receptionist's office. Gupta was told that he must remove the books from the office by 4 p.m. or face termination. A moving company relocated the boxes to his garage. With the help of another employee, Gupta sorted the books by state. Commodore told them they could work on their own time, and the company would consider buying the list from them. When the list was completed, Gupta gave Commodore two options; Pay $9,000 for exclusive rights to it, or receive it free of charge and permit Gupta and his partner to sell it to Commodore's competitors. Balking at the $9,000 cost, Commodore chose the later option. Gupta borrowed $100 from the Ralston Bank and invested the money in mailers which he then sent to other mobile home manufacturers. Within three weeks, he received checks for $22,000 and orders for another $13,000. Vinod Gupta had found his niche.

Hiring two part-time employees, Gupta launched American Business Information in 1972. The Omaha company created lists from the information available in telephone books. These lists became cost-saving marketing tools for mobile home manufacturers that needed sales prospects, and Gupta quit working for Commodore in 1973.

It took 13 years, but in 1986, ABI finally had the entire Yellow Pages in its database, ready to be accessed in any form that customers wanted. Gupta, however, continually plowed back the profits into his growing business to meet the increasing demands of his customers. Today *info*USA compiles and maintains a comprehensive database of information on ten million U.S., and one million Canadian businesses, and plans to create its own database of 115 million U.S. households.

ROBERT DAUGHERTY

Robert "Bob" Daugherty founded Valmont Industries, an international manufacturer of agricultural (primarily irrigation) equipment and industrial products, such as steel poles, pipe and tubing. Born in 1922, Bob Daugherty was 18 when World War II broke out. Like many of his peers, Bob entered the military and served with the Marines until the war ended. Upon returning to Nebraska, the 24-year-old Daugherty looked for a good business opportunity. He crossed the path of Sam McCleneghan, who owned a small manufacturing company named Valley Manufacturing, situated in a single farm building just west of Valley, Nebraska. Bob took his entire savings, $5000, bought the business, and began building farm elevators.

Before long, Valley Industries signed a contract with Sears Roebuck to build farm elevators. Over the course of the next few years, several 1,000 elevators were delivered to Sears to resell. To its product line the company soon added speed jacks, wagon hoists, universal joints, stalk cutters, and a front loader. When a recession hit the farm economy in 1952, Bob knew that his young company must diversify in order to survive.

While seeking a survival plan, Bob came in contact with Frank Zybach, a part-time farmer and inventor who had developed a fairly crude prototype of an agricultural irrigation machine that pivoted around a center post. Cumbersome at first, this contraption soon revolutionized Midwestern agriculture. During the next several years, Zybach continued to modify and refine his basic design. In 1954, he agreed to license his patent to Daugherty and Valley Manufacturing.

Center Pivot Irrigation

Valmont's engineers took Zybach's unit apart and spent the next several years making it sturdier, taller and more reliable. By the early 1960s, according to Daugherty, Valmont had overcome most of the design and production problems and had changed the original water hydraulic power system to electric drive.

Other "firsts" followed and reinforced Valmont's leadership role in the area of irrigation equipment. Hot-dip galvanizing was begun in 1966, providing long-term corrosion protection. The company also extended the life of each system with the introduction of high-quality drive train components, the most expensive part of the system. Since 1974, Valmont has built its own gearbox, which other pivot systems utilize as a replacement part.

Valmont Industries – Early 1960's

In 1959, Valmont began manufacturing steel pipe and tubing. They found that it wasn't always easy to get the pipe they required when they needed it, so they decided to make their own. From that beginning, the company saw an opportunity to manufacture not only pipe for its irrigation systems, but also to develop markets throughout the United States for use in both private and public projects.

Valmont continued to develop and refine a number of types of irrigation equipment, and currently operates from 27 facilities located in nine countries in North America and around the world, employing over 5,000 people worldwide. Today, over 15 million acres are irrigated by Valmont equipment in the U.S. and 90 other countries.

CHAPTER 5

CHUCK DURHAM

Chuck Durham was born in Chicago, Illinois in September of 1917. The world was engaged in World War I and his father, Jack Durham, was away at war when Chuck was born. Chuck's father survived the war and returned safely. Soon after his return, Jack Durham moved his wife and family to Iowa. Jack Durham was a civil engineer and worked for the State Highway Commission where he built roads in various parts of Iowa. During Chuck's formative years, they moved quite a bit. Chuck's father gave him a great deal of insight and exposure to the world of engineering and all of the efforts involved in the construction of roads. It is probably no coincidence that the histories of Walter Scott, Pete Kiewit and Peter Kiewit Sons', Inc. all involve the construction of roads. In elementary school Chuck took up a paper route. Every morning he would get up and deliver the papers at 5 o'clock and if you've ever been in central Iowa in January and February you know the devotion it takes to deal with such climatic conditions. This job would be an early indicator of Chuck Durham's work ethic.

Chuck went on to become an Eagle Scout and his commitment to this organization is reflected in the fact that he and his late wife, Marge, have made major contributions to the Omaha area Boy Scouts. Chuck's mother was a Catholic and his father was an Episcopalian so eventually Chuck ended up in a Congregational Church which was not too far from home. Chuck has said that he is proud of the fact that in his formative years he had a paper route, shoveled snow in the winter, and mowed lawns in the summer, and therefore never had to ask his parents for spending money. He completed high school in Iowa. Being the tall individual that he was, he tried his hand at tennis and performed quite well.

Chuck's father and grandfather were both engineers. Iowa State was near his home. Chuck said that his dad often joked that he could go to any school in the United States as long as it was located in Ames, Iowa. About the time he was entering college, the Great Depression came along. But, as was the case with a number of individuals in this book, his father was less effected by the economics of the Depression due to his job with the State Department of Roads.

In 1940 Chuck left Ames, Iowa and came to Omaha. He got a job working for $3 per day as a "flunky" in the drawing room at a company called Henningson Engineering Company. This would prove to be somewhat prophetic in that the owner of the company was the son of a hard working Danish immigrant named Henning H. Henningson, the father of Marge Henningson Durham.

Over the years, Chuck's abilities and standing with the company grew and eventually, the name of the company would be changed to Henningson, Durham, and Richardson. During the 40s and the 50s HDR became involved in many of the same construction projects as Peter Kiewit Sons', Inc. One of the company's most significant events occurred in 1976 with the formulation of an employee stock ownership trust. It gave all qualified employees the opportunity to share in the ownership of the company. It was also in 1976 that, after 27 years as president and chairman, Chuck Durham was succeeded by Bob Crone as president and CEO, while Chuck remained active as the Chairman of the Board. This stock ownership program was very similar in nature to that which was in place at Peter Kiewit Sons', Inc. The firm and its revenues continued to grow and in 1983, HDR was sold to a French firm, Bouygues. At this time, Chuck took the funds that he received from the sale of the company and began making various investments in a variety of businesses. From that day forward, he was able to create the wealth that he is now in the process of returning to the community.

MIKE YANNEY

Michael B. (Mike) Yanney does not fit neatly into either the Old Guard or the New Guard. He represents a mix of the old and the new. In terms of his age, he would come at the younger end of the Old Guard's generation, but his company is much newer than those of the Old Guard. Yanney was born in Kearney, Nebraska in 1935, during the height of the Great Depression. Kearney is a small city of about 27,000 located on the plains of central Nebraska. During the Depression, the population of Kearney was only about 8,000, and there were only two ways to make a living: either you worked in something related to agriculture or you worked for the Union Pacific Railroad.

Yanney's father moved from Omaha to Kearney to work for the railroad. His mother, an immigrant from Lebanon, was a strong-willed person who was instrumental in shaping his character and values. She instilled in him the principle that people need to be honest with themselves as well as others.

Yanney graduated from the University of Nebraska at Kearney and then went on to the University of Wisconsin's School of Banking. He moved to Omaha in 1961 where he met and married his wife, Gail Walling Yanney. From 1977 to 1984, Mike Yanney owned and managed a variety of commercial banks.

Yanney is also the founder and chairman of America First Mortgage Investments, a real estate investment trust (REIT) created to invest in mortgage securities, such as those guaranteed by government agencies Fannie Mae (more than 65% of the REIT's portfolio), Ginnie

CHAPTER 5

Mae, and Freddie Mac. America First manages 14 limited partnerships for over 100,000 individual investors around the world. The value of the assets controlled by the company is in excess of $3.5 billion. The company investments include multifamily real estate, mortgage companies, and agribusiness in Russia, along with other investments.

Mike Yanney dresses more colorfully than many business leaders in the Midwest, adding a colorful tie or pocket puff to the usual dark suit. Even his office makes use of color and bold patterns in contrast to the use of heavy wood so common in corporate offices.

Yanney's approach to business is straightforward and consistent with the views held by the majority of the Omaha mega-millionaires. He feels that success in business requires credibility, integrity, and dedication to taking care of those with whom you do business.

It also requires that you do the basics well and practice them over and over. To him, business is analogous to football. Winning in football requires constant practice and full attention to the basic part of the game: blocking and tackling. To Yanney and many like him, business is a game – a game where you keep score in dollars. Yanney enjoys the gamesmanship of business and has not been afraid to take the necessary risks. In contrast, Mike Yanney's older brother is more conservative and is not an entrepreneur. Even though they have the same parents and grew up in the same environment, they approach life quite differently. Neither Yanney nor his brother are old enough to have experienced the Great Depression first hand but they were shaped by the impression it left on their parents. Mike Yanney told me that he wanted to always have enough money so that he wouldn't have to worry about another depression. His brother, on the other hand, is very conservative and does nothing that would risk his money. Yanney began investing in Russian companies in 1977, when Russia was still the Soviet Union. As I listened to this story, I thought that no one I know would take that size of risk and know how to manage it.

In 1986, Yanney founded a youth mentoring program called All Our Kids, Inc. The program matches adult members of the community with students from the local junior and senior high schools. The adults serve as role models and support for the kids who are mostly from single parent homes.

Not all those who become wealthy through the creation of successful businesses remain in the ranks of the mega-millionaires. People often seem to choose their level of income. Once they have achieved a certain level, they may decide not to go further, or they change their focus. For whatever reason, not everyone may aspire to be a mega-millionaire, and of those who aspire to it, not everyone will make it. Let's look at a businessman who was successful but who does not fit the profile I have been developing. It may help to see what a mega-millionaire is, by seeing what one is not.

WILLIE THIESEN

Any discussion of the fast food business in Omaha must include the story of Willie Thiesen, an entrepreneur whose profile does not match that of most of the other mega-millionaires in this book. Thiesen is the one member of this group who made it to the ranks of mega-millionaire and then left them.

In the late 1960s Thiesen was on his way to California and decided to stop in Omaha. "I found I liked it here, " he would later recall. He made some friends and decided to stay. He worked in real estate for a while and then in 1973, he opened a place called "Wild Willie's Saloon" in a strip mall in southwest Omaha. His neighbor in the mall sold pizza, which was, at that time, a relatively new item for Midwestern Americans. The two business owners thought it might be a good idea to sell pizza to Willie's bar patrons. They merged their businesses. Since the *Godfather* movie and its sequels were popular then, they named the newly merged business "Godfather's Pizza," while still operating under different ownership.

One thing that Thiesen had in common with the other mega-millionaires was his ambition and his desire to build on an original idea. He worked relentlessly and began selling franchises for his restaurants. By 1983, Godfather's had over 900 outlets. At that point General Mills offered him $120 million dollars for the company and Thiesen sold it to them.

While Thiesen shared the ambitions of the other Omaha millionaires but his approach to life contrasts with theirs. At first, Thiesen invested his money, but later he showed a tendency towards conspicuous consumption not in keeping with the general unostentatious nature of the Omaha entrepreneurs. Thiesen spent money on cars, houses, and entertainment to a noticeable degree. He built an eighteen thousand square foot gated mansion in the well-to-do Regency district of Omaha. For his fortieth birthday he took ninety of his "closest" friends to London on the Concorde. In his heyday he had a Lear jet and I have heard rumors that he used it to fly over to Lincoln from Omaha (a hop of 60 miles). If true, it probably took him more time to land the plane than to fly the distance – or to drive. Thiesen also liked fast sports cars and at one time owned a Ferrari F40.

Unlike many of the other Omaha mega-millionaires, who tend to live relatively quiet lives and stay married to their original spouses, Thiesen has been married several times. While Nebraska is not a community property state, property acquired during a marriage does create a marital estate that must be divided "equitably" or fairly between the parties. In any event, entering into marriages and getting divorced is an expensive proposition no matter how it is done. It is certainly possible that his multiple marriages substantially depleted his net worth.

After his most recent divorce, Thiesen and his former wife had a large sale or auction, disposing of some significant luxury items such as a 15 inch crystal Baccarat horse head, a 19th century French mirror, and a pair of citrine falcons with diamond eyes. At the present time he would still be classified as well-to-do, perhaps even a millionaire, and at one point he resided in an apartment complex near the Regency neighborhood where he once owned the largest house. But he probably would not be considered one of the mega-millionaires at this time.

It comes down to a question of values – what you want to do with your wealth and how you want to do it. Mr. Thiesen enjoyed his wealth and still enjoys it, but probably has not amassed the legendary amounts of some of the other mega-millionaires described in this book.

In contrast, the next section describes one of Omaha's most successful mega-millionaires, Walter Scott.

WALTER SCOTT

As Chairman Emeritus of Peter Kiewit Sons', Inc., Walter Scott is Omaha's "other Billionaire." Peter Kiewit, Sr. founded the company before the Depression. In 1914, the senior Kiewit died and eventually Peter Kiewit, Jr. became head of the construction business. The company tried to survive the Great Depression by bidding on New Deal public work projects and via the transition into heavy and highway work. Survive it did. It also grew and prospered. Today's billion-dollar-plus annual revenues place it among the country's 10 largest construction companies. But today it represents a more diverse operation with activities in telecommunications, mining and energy generation. The Scott family's connection with the Kiewit company began in 1926 when Peter Kiewit hired Walter Scott, Sr. to supervise the construction of the tower on the Nebraska State Capitol in Lincoln. The senior Scott went on to become a Kiewit executive and later a Member of its board.

Born and raised in Omaha, young Walter spent summers in his youth as a laborer at Kiewit construction sites. His father's engineering interests led him to Colorado State University and an engineering degree, followed by an engineering job at Peter Kiewit Sons', Inc. As a young engineer, Walter moved up through the corporate ranks, not because of his connections, but because of his skill, effort and loyalty to the company. During those early years, he and his first wife, Carolyn, moved 17 times, the last time to the company's struggling Cleveland district, where Walter was a manager. Walter's original goal during this period was to gain the skill and resources to start his own construction company. In 1964, Peter Kiewit brought him back to Omaha, offered him new challenges and responsibilities, securing Walter's future with the company. Five years after Walter returned to Omaha, Bob Wilson took over as president, while Peter Kiewit remained as chairman.

During the next 10 years, Wilson's heart problems periodically kept him from the office. During these periods, Walter took over. In September 1979, Wilson resigned from the company. Two months later, Kiewit died. Scott became president and chairman as well.

As if this wasn't enough change in his life, Scott's wife was diagnosed with cancer within months of Kiewit's death. For almost four years Walter Scott arranged his schedule in order to spend more time at home with his family. Following her death, Scott devoted himself to a number of other activities, one of which led to his marriage with his second wife, Suzanne. Walter Scott headed the zoo foundation's board and Suzanne entered as the foundation's first Executive Director. The relationship grew and in 1987 they were married at the Countryside Community United Church of Christ. One aspect of Scott's life that separates him from many of the other Omaha mega-millionaires lies in his visibility in the community. He has given leadership, time and money to a whole host of community projects, including the Josyln Art Museum, the Henry Doorly Zoo, and the Peter Kiewit Institute of Information, Science, Technology, and Engineering which aspires to be one of the top ten such schools in the United States. The Peter Kiewit Institute was established with $23 million from the state and $47 million from local companies and individuals.

Being a billionaire makes you a member of a very small group. But over the years, Warren Buffett and Walter Scott have developed both a personal and a business relationship. They often attend University of Nebraska football games together. When Berkshire Hathaway sought listing on the New York Stock Exchange, it was required to have a director who was neither a Berkshire insider nor a Buffet family member. Buffett immediately turned to Scott. Berkshire Hathaway is also the only non-Kiewit company in the Kiewit headquarters building, Kiewit Plaza. Scott's fortune comes from his ownership of the stock of Peter Kiewit Sons', Inc., several related companies, and a substantial amount of commercial real estate. But it would be unfair to state that his fortune is simply the result of his Kiewit employment. During Walter's tenure at PKS, he has been diligent in maintaining the profitability of the firm's construction interests. He has been even more aggressive in moving the firm's assets and his personal assets into developing new businesses in young markets with tremendous growth potential. It should be noted that while his appetite for bigger and bigger challenges has resulted in huge personal financial reward, it has also created significant wealth for those fortunate enough to be associated with him. The bulk of this activity is centered into two areas: telecommunications and energy generation.

The energy involvement with Peter Kiewit Sons', Inc. and Walter Scott involves an energy company that was founded in 1971 and was originally named California Energy. It was founded to provide consulting and development services for geothermal power during the late 70s. The company recognized the many opportunities presented by the emerging industry deregulation in the United States and California Energy began to become a service provider as an independent power producer. Their original operations were centered in the Mohave Desert of Southern California. The basic operation was to find a pool of energy in the ground, mainly in the form of headed steam, and tap into that and as the pressure of the steam was relieved, it would power generators that created energy. Throughout the 70s and 80s the company continued to explore opportunities to provide geothermal power in the United States and they were actively seeking these types of geological situations in other parts of the world.

In 1991, Walter Scott and Peter Kiewit Sons', Inc. continued to explore places in which they could invest their cash flow and at this time they purchased an approximately one third position in the publicly traded shares of California Energy. Walter Scott then moved the headquarters to Omaha, Nebraska and put in charge of the operation a relatively young Omaha native by the name of David Sokol. Sokol is the son of a Safeway Manager in Omaha and David worked at the local supermarket to finance his college education at the University of Nebraska at Omaha. It was at the University of Nebraska at Omaha that David Sokol studied civil engineering and, as part of his education, he studied the profound ramifications that government deregulation of the power industry would have. Walter had a great deal of faith in Sokol and his vision about energy. Working with half of a billion dollars of outside investment, Sokol was able to transform the relatively small start up company of California Energy into a major international energy provider. Soon after Sokol took over, they changed the name to CalEnergy and became involved in the construction and operation of a number of geothermal operations in the Far East, primarily the

Phillipines and Indonesia. Kiewit was responsible for the construction of these operations and according to the contracts with the local governments, CalEnergy would be the ongoing operator.

Before Sokol began operations in the Far East he obtained political risk insurance from the overseas Private Investment Corporation, a U.S. government agency. This would serve to protect the company against expropriation by the governments of the countries in which they were operating. This turned out to be a fortunate choice when Indonesia reneged on power contracts it had with CalEnergy in the late 1990s.

One of the biggest accomplishments of CalEnergy occurred around 1996 when they were able to gain control of Northern Electric. This company was a major energy provider in the northern part of the United Kingdom, which, like the United States, was undergoing a great deal of deregulation of their former public utilities. The acquisition of Northern Electric provided CalEnergy management with valuable experience in operating in a newly deregulated environment. In 1999, CalEnergy announced that it had acquired MidAmerican Energy Holdings, one of the largest providers of energy services in the Midwestern United States. It includes operations in the Iowa, Illinois, Nebraska, and South Dakota. At that time, CalEnergy, having become MidAmerican Energy via the acquisition, was an international producer of energy.

The latest installment in the MidAmerican Energy saga came in late 1999 when it was announced that Berkshire Hathaway, in conjunction with Walter Scott and David Sokol, would purchase MidAmerican for approximately 9.3 billion dollars. The financial strength of Berkshire Hathaway and its better credit rating would help MidAmerican bring down borrowing costs and enhance its competitiveness as the energy industry continued on its deregulation path. Being part of Berkshire freed management from worrying about meeting Wall Street's expectations about smooth quarterly earnings growth. The deal was structured such that Berkshire Hathaway would own 75% of MidAmerican and Walter Scott and David Sokol would own the remaining 25% of the corporation.

Walter Scott and Peter Kiewit Sons', Inc. entered the communications business through a company called MFS. The company began in 1987 when a Kiewit executive by the name of Jim Crowe was looking for a new construction project. His unit was winding up its work on a fiber optic network for AT&T, MCI, and Sprint. Crowe told Scott that some investment groups were interested in building high capacity fiber optic loops in downtown business districts of Chicago and several other major cities in the interest of muscling in on the monopolies of the local

Bell Companies. The idea was to offer high volume business customers high quality inner building service and cheaper access to the long distance carrier by bypassing the local carrier. The Kiewit Board approved, but the one city project turned into two cities, three and so on. Soon, the Kiewit Board was writing checks for $5 or $10 million to fund new network construction of MFS. As time passed, the company continued in its rather aggressive growth pattern and revenues continued to grow, but by 1994 it became obvious that the company required additional capital in order to continue to grow. Peter Kiewit Sons', Inc. made a public offering with MFS in 1993 and in 1996, they sold the entire company to its Mississippi competitor, a company called WorldCom.

The style and personality of WorldCom CEO, Bernie Ebbers, clashed with that of Scott and Crowe. Crowe was chairman of WorldCom and Scott was a director. The two gentlemen soon resigned from WorldCom and returned to Kiewit. Around this time, there was a meeting of what Walter Scott calls "Our Gang." Every two years, Buffett invites about 30 top executives and their significant others to a multi-day retreat. In the summer of '95 they gathered near Dublin, Ireland and the topic was the internet. Bill Gates gave a presentation on the internet. It jarred Scott in a number of ways and got him thinking about a number of things. Gates told "Our Gang" that the internet was going to become far more significant than they realized and that he was repositioning Micosoft in order to meet the changes that the internet would provide. He also told Scott that the internet threatened the traditional phone powers by potentially taking away voice and data traffic. Scott later commented that if you weren't part of the revolution involving the internet, you were going to be sorely left behind.

Scott came back to Omaha, met with Jim Crowe, and they considered renewing the efforts that they had begun at MFS Communications. At this time, Kiewit had a small subsidiary called the Kiewit Diversified Group. It held Kiewit investments in a number of companies which included a small telecommunications company, CalEnergy, and a fairly extensive coal mining operation.

It was Scott's vision that this diversified group could become a next generation MFS and experience a fresh start. The business plan would be similar to the one that was already in place at MFS, but the technology would be the technology of the internet, therefore allowing the Diversified Group a significant technological leg up on all of its competitors. The diversified group would soon become Level 3 Communications.

Crowe and Peter Kiewit Sons', Inc. again began the process of building a new telecommunications network using fiber optics and switching systems based on IP (Internet Protocol). Level 3 Communications broke away from many of its other activities. CalEnergy was sold to the Berkshire group. Level 3 continued to grow and build its operations. The company was spun off from Kiewit in much the same way as Cal Energy. The Kiewit employees who held stock in Peter Kiewit Sons', Inc. received stock in both MFS and Level 3 Communications.

Today, Level 3 Communications continues to expand its operation by planting fiber optic cable under the Atlantic and Pacific Oceans and building networks around many of the major cities in Europe. Walter Scott continues to serve as Chairman of the Board of Level 3 Communications.

Scott's business interests are a prime example of how companies grow and diversify, and how the business of growing businesses becomes self-sustaining. No one starts out with huge companies, but those lucky or gifted few sometimes manage to create them.

To summarize: becoming a mega-millionaire requires the ownership of wealth-producing assets – in plain English – ownership of companies. The mega-millionaires in this book accomplished this by creating companies that may have started small, but grew. They took risks, reinvested the profits back into the company, and acquired other wealth-producing resources with those profits. They tend to live simply, with most of their wealth invested in capital-creating entities. What is amazing is that these are seemingly ordinary people whose companies are not cutting-edge technological innovators. They are companies that produce very typical products and services that anyone can make – and anyone can use. Most importantly, these individuals have a passion for the work they do. Most of them are no longer so much interested in money as they are interested in the game of money.

CHAPTER 6:
OLD GUARD, NEW GUARD: A CLOSER LOOK

The previous chapter provided an overview of several of Omaha's wealthiest individuals. But, in order to better understand just why and how a few people achieve such high levels of success as the Omaha mega-millionaires, I would like to examine the stories of two of them in particular: Peter Kiewit, founder of Peter Kiewit Sons', Inc., and Mike Simmonds, founder and owner of Simmonds Restaurant Management. I chose these two individuals because I believe their stories accurately represent those of the "Old Guard" and "New Guard." By presenting their stories together, I intend to illustrate some of the commonalities and differences among these two groups.

In 1884, Peter's father (also Peter Kiewit) and his Uncle Andrew, went into business for themselves. However, Andrew devoted some of his time to the management of the father's brick business because his father had become involved in a small meat market. Andrew and Peter, Sr. called their business, Kiewit Brothers. The business progressed modestly for the next several decades. Then, in 1912, Peter, Sr. and Peter's brothers, Ralph and George, formed a partnership known as Peter Kiewit and Sons. However, after two years of being bedridden, the father passed away in 1914.

Peter was only a teenager at the time of his father's death and Ralph became both father and big brother to him. Peter devoted much of his spare time helping out where ever he could in his brother's business. He performed any unskilled job where help was needed. He graduated from Central High School in 1918, while the U.S. was still involved in WWI. From here, a program similar to what we know today as ROTC, led him to Dartmouth University. By the end of his freshman year, the war had ended and he decided to return to Omaha and the construction business.

By this time, the business had changed its name to Peter Kiewit Sons. Peter worked there, but had not yet been made a partner. George became restless and in 1924, sought new opportunities and moved to San Diego. George's departure placed more and more responsibility on Peter's shoulders although he was only 23 at the time.

The company grew and prospered to the point it landed its first million-dollar contract: the ten-story Livestock Exchange Building in South Omaha. Peter Kiewit Sons landed several other significant projects in the late '20s. They built the tower for the Nebraska State Capitol building in 1927, Joslyn Art Museum in 1928, and the Omaha Union Pacific Railroad station in 1930, all outstanding examples of classic Art Deco architecture.

During this time Kiewit developed a system of cost accounting that enabled him to know the financial status of each project on a weekly basis. He saw early on that contractors didn't know they were in trouble until it was too late. But Kiewit required his foreman to turn in a record of costs every week so they could be compared to the estimated costs, and as head of the company he could zero in on any potential problems.

It was during the construction of the state capital building that Kiewit drove to Lincoln, Nebraska and met Walter Scott, Sr., a former University of Nebraska surveying instructor. Scott was working for another contractor when Kiewit recruited him. Scott would later become Kiewit's second in command and a director of the firm. Walter Scott was the first graduate engineer to work for the company and the father of Walter Scott, Jr.

In 1930, Kiewit's brother, Ralph, who was growing more conscious of the fact that the senior Kiewit died young, decided to leave the firm. At the time Ralph left, Peter Kiewit owned a quarter of the company stock and dissolved the company and reorganized it as Peter Kiewit Sons', Inc. The new firm had assets of $125,000 and it was about this time that the company's philosophy of employee ownership came into being. Peter intended that key employees become shareholders, but with the provision that the stock would be repurchased if they left the firm. He felt that the ownership of company stock would encourage these individuals to take a greater interest in the growth and financial success of the company. The philosophy of employee ownership was important to the development of the Kiewit Company and contributed to the development of the Omaha mega-millionaire group.

By now the 30-year-old Peter Kiewit was the majority shareholder and president of the company. It was also 1931 and the country was beginning to sink into the Depression and much of the economic activity in the country was beginning to slow down. Yet, during the Depression, Kiewit assembled a core group of talented people who would later help him build his company into one of the leading construction firms in North America.

During the Depression, the United States Federal Government took the Keynsian approach that the way to recharge the economy was to put as many people as possible to work on Government projects. Peter Kiewit Sons', Inc. became very active in bidding for and eventually building many roads in the upper plains region. In 1939, as the nation's leaders were making preparations for possible involvement in World War II, Kiewit received a $7.5 million contract to build 760 barracks at Fort Lewis, Washington. It was the company's largest contract ever and was also the most distant project from its Omaha headquarters.

By the end of World War II, the company had been involved in many war-related projects in the northern plains area. Because of these successes, the company was able to gain a major position both financially and in terms of the key personnel needed to move into the post war era. Because of the jobs they completed during the Depression, they were in a position to secure contracts to build the Interstate Highway system during WWII. They then emerged from the war as one of the major highway builders in the country. By the 1950's Kiewit had completed more miles on the interstate system than any other contractor and *Forbes* magazine produced an article about Peter Kiewit's success, calling him the "colossus of roads."

Peter died in 1979, and at the time of his death he was one of the wealthiest individuals in Nebraska. Much of his net worth became a part of the Peter Kiewit Foundation, which today has grown into an organization with assets in the neighborhood of about a half a billion dollars. For many years, the Kiewit Foundation has been instrumental in changing the face of Omaha. Not only is it providing funding for many local projects, but it is also providing leadership and direction in the community.

Even more important than the history of the company is what Peter Kiewit the man was about. He was dedicated to excellence and hard work, and he embodied the vision, values and work ethic that are the key to understanding the Omaha mega-millionaire population. Let's turn now to Mike Simmonds.

Mike Simmonds was born in Los Angeles approximately fifty years ago. His parents immigrated here from the British Isles, and as a child, Simmonds attended the usual public elementary and secondary schools in Southern California. I was growing up in Southern California at about the same time and life in the 1950s and 1960s was typical of prosperous America of that era, with the addition of perpetual good weather. Southern California was a great place to grow up.

Simmonds's father ran a retail shoe store and he has warm memories of him, in spite of the fact that his father worked six and often seven days a week for long hours in his business. He admired his father for his devotion to his family and his work and has relied upon him as a role model in his own life. However, Simmonds has gone far beyond his father's success in the successes of his own business, as we shall see shortly.

After completing high school, Simmonds attended Pasadena City College for a short time, but did not seem to possess any driving ambition and was uncertain what direction his future would – or should – take. The Vietnam War was underway and Simmonds was drafted into the army. After boot camp, he was sent to Georgia and there he was assigned to the chaplain and spent part of his time driving kids to the beach. He was eventually transferred to Alabama, and it was while he was in Alabama that he met his wife, Lynn, at a party. Their marriage has been a strong one, a fact in which he takes great pride, that has given his life a stability that he would probably agree is important to any kind of success.

Shortly after his marriage, Simmonds enrolled at the University of Alabama and made an effort to complete his college education. While he was in college he took a job part time working for a Burger King in Decatur, Alabama, and began training to be the night manager. Simmonds speaks very fondly of Fred Wessel, the franchise owner at that time. He said that Wessel was an important mentor and inspired him to continue working in the business. From this mentoring relationship, Simmonds began to develop strong ideas about how business should be conducted. Wessel felt very strongly that his restaurants and their employees must provide the best quality product that was possible for the price. He demanded that the restrooms be clean, the facilities tidy, and the service as prompt as possible. He believed that if all of these guidelines were followed, that customers would go away with a good feeling about their experience. This may sound trite, but it isn't. Most successful restaurants and food chains stress the importance of quality and service. The ones that don't hold to these vital qualities simply don't survive. There is no question that Simmonds was greatly influenced by the example of his father's hard work and the mentoring of his first employer, Fred Wessel. From Wessel, Simmonds learned that the customer expects fast food to be more than just "fast." He learned that the employees must execute accuracy, quality, and friendliness for each and every customer.

Eventually Simmonds was able to complete his college education and he found that he still had a great interest in the fast food restaurant business. Her sought to buy a franchise from Burger King and was offered one in West Virginia and one in Fremont, Nebraska, which is a rather small community approximately 30 to 40 miles northwest of Omaha.

Simmonds and his wife, who was a teacher, knew early on that they wanted to become Burger King franchise owners. So they saved all of his Lynn's salary and when the time was right, they took all of the cash that they had from her salary and the equity from their home and put down approximately $40,000 for the purchase of the franchise. This was in 1976, and the Simmonds chose Nebraska, moved to Fremont, and started the operation. They had planned and worked together, saved that nest-egg, and now were ready to begin building what would become a fast-food empire. But they started, as anyone starts, at the beginning, with one restaurant.

In the beginning Lynn participated somewhat in the business, but Simmonds was the real head of the operation. Simmonds is proud of his business and told me that with the first franchise he would sit there and he would watch them making hamburgers and he was very concerned with the pattern in which the pickles were laid upon the bun and wanted to make sure the swirl of catsup was absolutely perfect so with every bite you got a bite of catsup and there was no bite of the hamburger that was without it. This pride in one's work is a very important and very telling trait. No one will be successful unless they care, and care a great deal, about what they do. It doesn't matter what the business is, but you must care about it and take pride in it or it will not do well.

After several years in Fremont, Simmonds had an opportunity to purchase some additional franchises in Omaha and this he did. Eventually, approximately half the franchises in Omaha were owned by Simmonds and the other half were actually company stores. By that I mean they were owned and operated by Burger King, the parent company. In the following chapter, we will examine these arrangements in greater detail.

CHAPTER 6

One of the elements that went into Simmonds's decision to choose Nebraska was that he felt the work force in this area had a stronger work ethic than that which existed in other parts of the country. He believed that his philosophy of hard work and pride in one's work would find fertile ground here, and that he would have no trouble finding a staff who would not be afraid to work hard and who would help make his business the best that it could be.

Approximately fifteen years ago, Simmonds was offered the option to purchase all of the company stores in Omaha, which he did. He felt that it was important to him and the business to do this if he could, because the two sets of operations had different policies, different price structures, and advertising, and he did not want consumers to receive mixed messages. When Simmonds was able to purchase the remaining stores, he would standardize all of the Burger King outlets in the community, which he believed helped to create a more positive and consistent image of the Burger King product. Today, Simmonds owns approximately 72 Burger King restaurants in Omaha and Des Moines.

I find it interesting that several years ago Simmonds decided that, rather than being the hands-on manager of the corporation and its day-to-day activities, he needed to step back and find a president who would take care of the daily operations. Simmonds recognized that this shift of roles would allow him to focus on the big picture more clearly. This trait is typical of many successful entrepreneurs. They developed a project successfully, and then feel comfortable handing off the maintenance to others. In turn, the entrepreneur is free to move forward to new challenges.

While he did not do this by design, it is interesting that the individual Simmonds chose to manage his Midwestern Burger King empire is a former banker, Paula Glissman. Incidentally, Paula is not the only woman in the upper echelons of the organization. Numerous division managers, the head of Human Resources, and the Vice Presidents of Training and Operations are also women. It is interesting to note further that the President of Burger King USA is also a woman. These choices did not arise necessarily by design, but rather, they were the result of working with the people he knew and with whom he felt comfortable in the operation of his business.

Now, let's look at some of the business traits and shared values that these two successful business men exemplify, in order to see how the New Guard and Old Guard match up. Has the New Guard been forced to radically modify the Omaha way of living and doing business in order to compete in today's environment? I hope that one of the things you picked up from the stories of Peter Keiwit and Mike Simmonds was that their first job was their last job. Kiewit was in the same business all his life and there is a good possibility that the same will be true for Simmonds. This is not to say that an individual must stay in the same job all of his or her life, but, in both cases, these men found fairly early on something they wanted to do, to succeed in, to have ownership of. Their careers are more than just jobs. Simmonds would not be content just to work in a Burger King, even as a manager. He knew early on that he wanted to be a franchise owner and worked to reach that goal.

These people love what they do and they are relentless in their pursuit of a goal. They may or may not know precisely what that goal is: Simmonds may not have realized when he bought his first franchise where that ambition would take him. Clearly, successful business owners have a very strong desire to succeed and they put all of their energy and effort into achieving that success. They have an ongoing need to continue to build and they do not quit building. They may move on to different projects once they reach a certain level of success, but they cannot conceive of just stopping.

To use the examples I have relied on here, there are many people in the construction and the fast food industries who reach a certain size and level of success and who seem to be content with that. They stop expanding, growing, and changing their businesses. But neither of the two men discussed in this chapter felt that way. They are action-oriented. My observation is that it is not a sense of discontent that drives them, but rather, it is a need they have to continue to face new challenges. I think it was Jack London who said, "I would rather wear out than rust out."

Another theme of this book, and one that is true of these two entrepreneurs, is that both of them took businesses that were fairly plain-jane businesses and made them very successful. Over the years, the accomplishments of Peter Kiewit Sons', Inc. have put them in the upper end of their peer group. As mentioned earlier, when Kiewit was running the company back in the mid 30s and early 40s, most of the projects with which they were involved were awarded on a bid basis. So, in order to get the job, it was very important to come up with a very low estimate of the cost of doing a project. From a financial point of view, the problem with this is that by providing the service at the lowest cost, it is difficult to achieve significant profitability. Kiewit recognized the problem of the narrow range of profitability inherent in his business. One of the character traits people like Kiewit possess is the ability to recognize that they do not need to simply accept a certain set of circumstances and move on. Rather, they are much more inclined to develop an entirely new way of operating. They see this as a challenge, they respond to the challenge, and they find a way of making things better.

Kiewit's response to this problem was to avoid or minimize losses by careful management. This approach to running a construction business has contributed greatly to the firm's success. Kiewit Company's efficiency also illustrates another point: good business requires a commitment to the long term. Day-to-day operations cannot be sloppy and they cannot be inconsistent. A commitment to consistency and quality over time is one of the key factors that produces extraordinary results. In this day of hurry up, come-and-get-it, this point may fall upon deaf ears. But there are few overnight successes. True success is measurable and long lasting. True success lies in the ability to respond to problems in a creative, productive way, in commitment to long-term performance, and in pride in one's work.

Peter Kiewit Sons', Inc. started to diversify their company as early as the 1950's. Eventually, they owned a data processing firm, a construction firm, an electrical utility company, and a startup telecommunications company. This diversification was another factor that contributed to the firm's financial success and has been instrumental in the creation of a great deal of wealth in Omaha. Likewise, Mike Simmonds has taken his business model for his fast food operation and adjusted in a wide variety of ways. As a result, the value of his company has grown at a rate that exceeds many of its peers. In the following chapter on public and private companies, I will go into additional detail about how these two gentlemen approach their businesses.

Another area where successful individuals from the Old Guard and New Guard excel is in their ability to choose personnel. In general, they seem to have an ability to sense the nature of the people that they hire. They seek out the qualities in others that are similar to their own personal qualities. They have a knack for unearthing the drive to exceed average expectations. They expect a great deal from the people who work with them and for them. In the old days, when Pete Kiewit was alive, it was widely known that you were expected to be in the office at least part of the day on Saturday and long hours were the rule, rather than the exception.

Another practice that successful individuals employ is the consistent recognition of excellence in their managers and their tendency to delegate responsibility without reservation. They are not micro-managers. They give each individual very broad guidelines of what is expected of them and inform them of their expectations. This is an incredibly important characteristic in creating a company that is financially successful because it operates on the understanding that each member of the company should be thoroughly engaged with the aspect of the job that they know best. By delegating authority when it should be delegated, you create the opportunity to use your own time and talent more effectively, as well as those of your employees. If a company owner must supervise his management, the result is, more often than not, two people doing one job. Obviously, this kind of approach is not very efficient and limits the opportunities of the owner to develop new venues or pursue new opportunities for growth.

Throughout the Old Guard and the New Guard, one can see the ability of company leaders to pick the right people and let them do their job. But that represents only half of the skill. They are also highly skilled at motivating their employees. One practice that they have in common is to invite the key people in both of these organizations to participate in the growth of the value of the company. This is a model that Pete Kiewit actually started back in the mid-1930s when he encouraged managers to buy shares in the company. It worked for a variety of reasons. First, it forced individuals to save in a time when the importance of saving had become painfully apparent. Secondly, being part owners in the company created for the employees a strong personal interest in the financial growth and wellbeing of the company.

Simmonds has also taken the opportunity to provide shares of his equity in his business to his key company people. This practice informs the employees that they are a part of the team and are important to the company, and it also gives them an incentive to foster the financial growth and wellbeing of the company.

In many ways, the traditions of the Old Guard are being carried out in the work of the New Guard. Over the years, an innovative, flexible approach to business and strong, active leadership have led to the creation of many successful companies and a thriving financial community.

CHAPTER 7: PUBLIC AND PRIVATE

The previous chapter presented a comparison between a representative of the Old Guard and one of the New Guard. Now, we will narrow our focus a bit to examine the differences between publicly held and privately held companies. Then, we will look at two specific examples of business practices held by several of the Omaha mega-millionaires, practices that served to increase the productivity of their companies. In earlier chapters I have noted that these companies produced fairly ordinary products and services that could not be classified as "high-tech." To elaborate, they are not companies on the leading edge of the kind of scientific innovation that seeks to profoundly alter the lives of humankind. *They are companies that do what they do exceptionally well.*

It is important to understand what it means to perform exceptionally well. Management and shareholders can evaluate their companies by employing many different systems of measurement. That is to say, success or financial soundness can be measured in different ways. Some companies measure their success by how large a share of the market they control for their product. Others evaluate their success by how rapidly they are increasing the number of stores they have. Some technical companies evaluate themselves by how many inventions or scientific breakthroughs they come up with in a year. These things are all well and good, and all will provide a certain amount of information about how well a company is doing. But the primary reason for being in business is to make money. Naturally, many of the Omaha companies tend to focus on the bottom line or profitability, or, how much is left over after paying the bills.

Among these companies are engineering firms, trucking firms, insurance firms, retailers, fast food providers, and others who provide their customers with high quality goods and services of a very familiar sort.

Omaha is home to four, Fortune 500 companies. These include ConAgra, Berkshire Hathaway, Mutual of Omaha, and Peter Kiewit Sons', Inc. Of the 500 largest corporations in the world, two are headquartered in Omaha. This includes ConAgra, a mutli-faceted food conglomerate that, on a revenue basis, is larger than Coca-Cola and Berkshire Hathaway. The index of Nebraska stocks has exceeded both the Dow and the Standard & Poor's 500 for the last eight years.

As I have mentioned several times, the wealth amassed by the Omaha mega-millionaires comes from their ownership of companies, not from incomes or inheritance. Most of the mega-millionaires started the companies that made them wealthy. The majority of this total wealth is in companies that are publicly traded. However, there are several fairly large companies in the group that are privately held. Publicly traded means that shares representing ownership of the company are bought and sold in the open market where anyone with the money can buy them. Privately held indicates that ownership is restricted to one individual or a very small group such as a family.

The fact that so much of the Omaha wealth is held in publicly traded companies has some profound ramifications. The owner of a privately held company is free to run the company in any way that he or she pleases and is not concerned about the thoughts and needs of any partners. A privately held company also frees the owner from having to disclose anything about the financial nature of the company to the general public. Obviously, owners must report to the state and national tax authorities, but not to the local paper. A publicly traded company is required to report to, and hopefully please, the shareholders. It also requires disclosure of financial information to shareholders, including information about the exact nature of management's participation in the company. Thus a portion of your finances becomes very visible. Not only is this information available to the specific shareholders of the company, but also to members of the financial community who provide advice to their clients. Thus, managers and owners of publicly traded companies are subject to more public scrutiny than their privately held counterparts.

Another significant difference between a publicly traded company and a privately held company lies in the pricing mechanism. Publicly traded companies are priced on a daily basis in a market, which, in the short term, is often irrational. This price represents the pushing and tugging feelings of the market based sometimes on reality but more often on perception. As a result of these market forces, the price that the market sets does not always reflect the financial reality of the company. At times the market can greatly overprice the underlying economic value of the company, and at other times, it can do exactly the opposite. This happened to Joe Ricketts, the founder of the discount brokerage firm, AmeriTrade. In early 1999, the publicly traded shares of AmeriTrade went from $5 to $42 in 4 months. During this period, Joe's net worth increased 750%. But during the course of the next year, the stock fell to $11, a decline of nearly 400%. Because privately held company stock is valued on the real assets of the firm and not the emotions of the investing public, they rarely experience these price swings. Privately held companies are rarely sold at irrational prices. This can be positive or negative, depending upon your side of the transaction. Consider Joe Ricketts. If he had sold all of his share of AmeriTrade when they went from $5 to $42, he would have received a considerable windfall due to the irrational state of the market. Had it gone the other way, he would have received far less than a reasonable price for his company.

The plus in owning publicly traded shares lies in their flexibility for transferring the assets to another entity or converting the assets to cash. This will play a major role in the future of Omaha. Since many of them, particularly the Old Guard, have their fortunes intact and don't intend to pass them on to their children, they will leave their money to society. Having their assets invested in publicly traded companies facilitates this process. They can pass shares of stock to a foundation, only passing a portion of the company ownership and assets, and management can remain in place. However, if it were a privately held company, they would have to gift the whole company, rather than giving away only a portion of it.

Below I have compiled a table that includes both the major publicly traded and privately held Omaha companies, including the businesses they are in and estimates of their annual revenues. Not all heads of the publicly traded companies belong on the mega-millionaire list. Several of the older companies have created wealth that is not concentrated in any individual.

MAJOR OMAHA PRIVATELY HELD COMPANIES

Company	Owner	Sales	Business
Scoular	Marshall Faith	$1.86B	Grain Trading
Peter Kiewit Sons', Inc.	Employee	$3.5 B	Construction
Lozier Corporation	Alan Lozier	$300M+	Store Fixtures
Omaha Steaks	Simon Family	$350M+	Gift Steaks
Oriental Trading Co.	Terry Watanabe	$200M+	Small Plastic Toys
Pacesetter Homes	Phil Schrager	$300M	Prefab Homes & Windows
HDR	Employee	$250M	Engineering
Omaha World-Herald	Employee	$250M	Newspaper
Gordman's	David Gordman	$220M	Retail
Simmonds Rest. Mgmt.	Mike Simmonds	$235M	Fast Food
Travel & Transport	Employee	$450M	Travel Agency
Millard Ref. Services	Larry Larson	$100M+	Wholesale Meats

The purpose of this list is to give you an impression of what these companies do and how large they are as measured by sales. They provide basic products, from agricultural products such as grain, to retail and wholesale outlets for a variety of products, to construction, design, and fast food. But I would like to emphasize that none of these products and services are "high-tech." Most of these products and services could have been produced at any time within the last fifty years. What is amazing is the success of what appears to be very ordinary types of businesses.

MAJOR OMAHA PUBLICLY TRADED COMPANIES

Company	Chairperson	Sales	Business
Acceptance Insurance	Mike McCarthy	$200M	Property Casualty Insurance
AmeriTrade	Joe Ricketts	$570M	Discount Brokerage
Ballantyne of Omaha	John Wilmers	$40M	Motion Picture Equipment
Berkshire Hathaway	Warren Buffett	$24B	Financial
Commercial Federal	Wm. Fitzgerald	$900M	Banking
ConAgra	Bruce Rohde	$26B	Food Processor
First National Bank	Bruce Lauritzen	$900M	Banking
infoUSA	Vinod Gupta	$300M	BusinessLists
Transaction Systems Architects	Wm. Fisher	$300M	Banking Software
Trangenomic	Collin D'Silva	N/A	Biotech
Union Pacific	Dick Davidson	$12B	Railroad
Valmont Industries	Mogens Bay	$800M	Irrigation, Lightning Poles
Werner Enterprises	Clarence Werner	$1.1B	Trucking
West Teleservices	Gary West/Troy Eaden	$650M	Telemarketing

The Omaha companies are quite successful. Still, their businesses are quite simple and ordinary. How can that be? Being in a simple, basic industry actually works in their favor. They enjoy reasonable profit margins because their position in the marketplace is not dependent upon the periodic development of new inventions or breakthrough innovations.

Those who make their fortune with new products or inventions have two potential problems to face. First, they are under constant pressure to keep up with the latest innovations. A company is only as good as its latest innovation, and there is always someone else who may build on a company's advances and outperform it. The computer and software industries face this problem continually. The second problem such companies face is that the investment a company must put into research and development in order to keep its competitive edge can be costly. The success of such companies is entirely dependent upon their ability to out-produce thier competitors. Ideally, when the final product reaches the consumers' hands, the company is then able to recoup its investment and then, in addition, see a profit. There is nothing wrong with businesses that do this, but they sometimes have a more difficult time staying ahead than businesses that do not seek to produce the latest innovation in a given industry.

Having seen a broad view of the Omaha companies, let's look at several ways in which the Omaha mega-millionaires have refined their methods of conducting business. I believe that small modifications in their business plans have resulted in significant differences in the bottom lines of their companies.

CHAPTER 7

Let's begin by turning our attention to the fast food industry. This industry exists in virtually every American city, with the possible exception of the most sparsely populated towns. The fast food operations in Omaha are familiar ones that include Wendy's, McDonald's, Arby's, and Burger King. On the surface, they all appear to be quite similar. Let's return to Mike Simmonds. An overview of his operation will lend better insight into the methods that distinguish Omaha's mega-millionaires from some of the rest.

Let's look at Burger King. From a bottom line perspective, Burger King holds an edge over some other fast food franchises. They serve three meals: breakfast, lunch, and dinner. This may seem like a trivial difference, but if a restaurant serves a menu that suits only two meals, it sits idle all morning. Assume that the construction costs for building a Burger King restaurant and a Taco Bell restaurant are identical. For four hours per day, Taco Bell is not generating revenue while Burger King is. Industry information that I have gathered supports this. The average Taco Bell location grosses $700,000 to $800,000 per year, while the Burger King average is slightly over $1,000,000.

Mike Simmonds is well aware of the fact that the first word in fast food is fast. He recognized that most people patronize fast food restaurants mainly because the food is available immediately. Fast food will never be equal to the food prepared from scratch in a Five-Star restaurant. One has to balance the quality of food with the speed with which it can be prepared. But then again, it is ready much faster, costs less, and tastes good. If fast food is poor quality, people will not return to eat it. But likewise, if fast food is good, but not fast, people in a hurry will not continue to patronize the business.

Simmonds has been involved in time and motion studies, particularly as they apply to the drive-up window, which is, of course, the hallmark of fast food restaurants nowadays. One has only to look at the drive-up window lines during any given lunch hour to witness their popularity. At one of his flagship shops at 114th and Dodge, the second busiest intersection in Omaha, Simmonds has two drive-up window lines. One person takes your order, another takes your money, and a third person gives you your food. Rumor has it that it is one of the fastest drive-up operations in the country.

Another area that distinguishes Mike's operations from the pack lies in his desire and ability to profitably expand the number of locations. There are many individual franchises across the nation that stop at 2, 3, and 4 locations. But the ability to profitably expand a fast food operation requires drive, determination, and the willingness to delegate and manage on a grander scale. The major difference between the Simmonds operation and much of the rest of the pack lies in the relationship between Simmonds Restaurant Management (the franchisee) and the parent Burger King Corporation (the franchisor).

The more traditional model is that followed by McDonald's, and is probably the most common. The arrangement between a McDonald's franchisee and the parent company is relatively simple. You approach the McDonald's corporation showing you have the financial wherewithal to go into the business. McDonald's will pick the sites for you, they will buy the land, they will build the buildings, get it all set for you to come in and open the door. You sell the food and the return on your investment consists of the monies from selling the fast food, minus your operating expenses.

For some individuals, this is a desirable arrangement. Virtually all of the problems of location, ownership and construction are taken off your hands and every month you simply pay rent to the McDonald's corporation for the use of their building. You purchase your raw products through their distribution mechanism and pay them a percentage of your gross sales. This affords you the right and privilege of being a McDonald's franchisee and you can then benefit from the name recognition of McDonald's. According to the McDonald's franchise model, the reward or return to the individual franchisees is simply the difference between what they take in at the restaurant and what they must spend for rent, payroll, raw materials, and the McDonald's Corporation franchise fee.

Burger King – 114th & Dodge Streets

CHAPTER 7

The relationship that the Simmonds Restaurant organization has with the parent Burger King Corporation is considerably different from that of the McDonald's model. Simmonds is free to choose his own sites, but he must go out and negotiate for the land, purchase it, and be responsible for all of the construction and maintenance that is involved. He also has an arrangement with the Burger King parent wherein he has some financial responsibility for, and limited control over, the time and place and content of his local advertising.

The McDonald's model obviously requires less effort on the part of the franchisee in order to establish the business. A great deal of the restaurant's functions are the responsibility of the national organization. Under the Burger King model, the franchisee is responsible for much more.

While operating within the Burger King Model requires more effort on the part of the franchisee, it can also provide him or her with a significantly greater return. If the franchisee buys the land and building with a mortgage and applies a portion of this cash flow to pay it off, the owner is going to build up equity in the business. And if the location is properly chosen, historical indications are that the appreciation return on real property will provide the owner an additional return on their investment. Thus, the owner operator of a franchise using the Burger King model has the potential to see a greater profit should he decide to sell the business. He pays out more in the beginning and perhaps takes more risks because of his larger initial investment, but if his business is successful, he may reap much greater rewards if he sells.

In order to make a clear distinction between the McDonald's model and the Burger King model, let's compare it to either renting or buying a house. The McDonald's franchise pays rent to the McDonald's corporation. In return, the renter gets use of the building and the land. But in doing so, they don't build any equity in either the business or the real estate. Should the McDonald's owner wish to sell the business, the sale price would be approximately 1.2 times the gross amount of the location's annual sales. So, if the McDonald's location had been grossing $1.2 million a year in sales, they could sell the business for 1.4 million. Over the years, the franchisee has paid X number of dollars to the McDonald's Corporation for the location and they enjoy no return on those dollars. The growth of their assets relies solely on what the franchisee did with any of the profits from the business. They could have put them in the bank or invested them in other locations but the rent money is gone.

On the other hand, under to the Burger King model, the owner takes out a loan to buy the land. Over the years, they pay themselves "rent," which is, essentially, payments that apply to the purchase of the land. The "rent" reduces the company's taxes because it is part of the cost of doing business. Over the years, as is the case with a house, the real estate of the Burger King franchise has appreciated in value. This could be due to its location and the fact that real estate grows with inflation because of the increase in replacement cost.

So, when the Burger King owner goes to sell his franchise location, the outcome is modified. First, as with the McDonald's owner, he can sell the business for approximately 1.2 times the annual gross sales. But, he also has a piece of real estate that has been paid for by the cash flow from the business and probably appreciated in value over time.

The Simmonds Restaurant Management has been both astute and lucky in the selection of their sites. For example, they have an operation at the corner of 114th and West Dodge Road in Omaha, which is a very busy intersection. Simmonds was able to purchase the land many years before the growth of the city of Omaha had reached this particular point, and he was thus able to buy at a fairly low price and see its value grow. Therefore, the return that the Simmonds Restaurant Management is able to get out of its properties makes the Burger King model a more profitable operation in the long run.

In addition to their financial skills, the Omaha mega-millionaires tend to be capable managers, and are good at motivating their employees to excel. One very obvious way to motivate employees is to offer them an opportunity to share in ownership of the company.

Let us turn once again to the work of Peter Kiewit and take a closer look at his management style then, and how that style carried through to the company's current operations. We know that he was good at choosing and motivating people. In the late 1930s and early 1940's he began a program of employee stock ownership in the company for his senior managers. First of all, this was a way of encouraging saving. The Kiewit investment program was not the same as the stock programs that are prevalent on Wall Street where top executives are given options to buy stock. Under the Wall Street model, managers buy company stock at highly discounted prices. Quite often, after they have purchased the discounted stock, they may sell it in the open market and realize an immediate, significant profit. In contrast, the Kiewit stock can only be owned by employees and they must pay book value for it. It must be sold back at book value if an individual leaves the company. Book value is the value of the real assets of the company. Secondly, by being owners of the company, Kiewit felt that the employees would work harder for the company, and be more concerned about its economic performance.

Peter Kiewit's belief that people should work hard and be frugal was an integral aspect of the Kiewit culture. During Pete's lifetime, and, perhaps, for several decades after his death, this model for employee motivation and an incentive to remain loyal to the company worked well. Peter Kiewit Sons', Inc. grew and prospered. Their financial results put them in the upper range of their peer group.

The 1990's presented a significant change in this program. It was during this time that Peter Kiewit Sons', Inc. became involved in the communications business through MFS and Level 3 communications. Due to some internal financial restructuring at Peter Kiewit Sons', Inc., many of the Kiewit shareholders became significant shareholders in MFS and Level 3 communications. Share prices for both of these companies rose dramatically during the technology boom that the stock market enjoyed in the late 1990's. As a result, many Kiewit employees went from being financially comfortable to having a net worth of 10, 20, and 30 million dollars in a relatively short period of time.

What followed was a major change in the motivation equation. Most of these individuals were not employees of Level 3 Communications. Consequently, their professional activities had no impact on the success or failure of the company. The loyalty factor was not present. In addition, a dramatically enthusiastic investing public drove up the share price of Level 3 Communications many fold.

Because of the dramatic increase in their net worth, some of them chose to take early retirement. I have talked to numerous residents of an upscale development in West Omaha who refer to a small section of their subdivision as the "Level 3 region." They believe that some houses in the region were financed by the sales of Level 3 Communications shares.

It is a question of how much is enough. Not everyone has the motivation to be an entrepreneur who reinvests and creates the wealth that Kiewit and others like him did. But for those who want to do it, the blueprint is plain to see. Start small, reinvest profits, work hard and smart at what you do well, and watch the results grow. It will take a number of years for your efforts to mature, but if these Omaha entrepreneurs can do it, anyone can.

It is plain to see that the face of Omaha's business community is diverse in its approach to business, with companies both public and private, and rich histories that have played out in a variety of ways. It will be interesting to see what direction the Omaha financial community will take in the future, when certain business practices continue to prove effective, and other practices recede in the face of more modern ones.

CHAPTER 8: FOR THE LOVE OF THE GAME

The character traits and attributes of the mega-millionaires reveal a great deal about how they achieved their success. Our culture tends to think that the rich are those who have important jobs or are celebrities who can command large salaries. These ideas about the rich are derived from famous athletes or movie stars, and high profile CEOs who may have incomes ranging from $10 million to $30 million or more a year. But the wealth of the Omaha mega-millionaires *is not about large incomes*. All the Omaha mega-millionaires are where they are today because they own all or part of a company. Most of the wealth they created consists of stock in a company they created, either public or private.

All of these individuals made their fortunes from the ownership of companies. In addition, the companies themselves have something in common. They all produce fairly ordinary goods and services. There are no high tech companies. None of the Omaha companies have "invented" anything. They have produced no medical or scientific breakthroughs. They do not produce complex electronic or industrial products. They are finance companies, construction companies, companies that sell plastic novelties and a company that copies phone numbers onto CDs. These companies that offer very basic products and services have one thing in common – they have significantly increased the net worth of their owners.

Bob Daugherty serves as an example of a somewhat more innovative approach to product. Daugherty started with a small company which he bought with his nest egg of life's savings and turned into a multi-million dollar corporation operating on a global scale. His company produced new and innovative products, but these were not technologically advanced products. Rather, they were products that presented better, more efficient ways of irrigating the land. So, along with the other mega-millionaires described in this book, Bob Daugherty represents a company that is not so unusual in what it produces, but is unusually successful at producing a rather ordinary product.

If you were to examine a photo gallery of our subjects, you would notice right away that all of them are male except for one. The exception is Rose, "Mrs. B." Blumkin, who, in 1935, started the nation's largest furniture store under one roof, Nebraska Furniture Mart. The fact that there is only one female member of this group can be partially explained in historical terms. The group described here began their businesses in the middle twentieth century, and women entrepreneurs were not common. When we look to the future, that picture may change, but for now, Mrs. B is the exception.

We know that there is a great deal of wealth in the Omaha community, but how does this wealth manifest itself in the lives of its owners? The Omaha mega-millionaires are seen by many Omaha citizens as frugal or even cheap because of their relatively modest lifestyles. In reality, they are not frugal. They are unostentatious. But the reason they live the way they do is not necessarily to save money. Rather, their values discourage conspicuous consumption. Numerous people have told me that Peter Kiewit, a leader and perhaps role model for the Old Guard, discouraged his managers from owning fancy cars or oversized homes. The top executives' offices at Kiewit were often small rooms with linoleum floors and metal desks.

I have spoken to many members of the Old Guard and a good portion of them appear to share this attitude. One individual who knows the Old Guard well is Willis "Bill" Strauss. For many years, Strauss headed the local natural gas utility, Northern Natural Gas. He is an Omaha native, educated in the Omaha schools and married to another Omaha native, and he is a prominent civic figure and leader. During my first interview with him he told me that it is just "plain socially unacceptable to flaunt your wealth in Omaha."

Likewise, Bill Fischer, who currently heads Transaction Systems Architect, Inc., made the following observation in my first interview with him. He said, "the Omaha wealthy felt that if you flaunted it, you would lose it."

While most of the members of this group have homes in Omaha that are quite modest in relation to their net worth, several of them own second and third houses in much more interesting and exotic places, such as Chuck Durham's house in San Francisco, Walter Scott's ranch in Wyoming, Joe Rickett's house in Wyoming or Warren Buffett's beach house in southern California. They may appear modest, but they enjoy some luxuries. They just don't flaunt their wealth at home. Further, based upon their net worth, the Omaha wealthy appear to spend a relatively small portion of their wealth.

It boils down to three things. First, being ostentatious in Omaha is not socially acceptable. Secondly, having big houses, flashy cars, etc., does not really appeal to members of this group. They are content with what they have. And thirdly, it is the nature of their assets that they don't have a disposable income proportionate to their wealth.

There is another way to view the same situation. I asked one of the original Buffett partners why he was giving away millions of dollars to public organizations instead of spending it on himself. His response was, "I already have everything I need." He has three houses, a boat and a Corvette. You can only be in one house at a time and drive one boat or one car at a time.

The fact that many of these individuals live in the same house all their lives is due to the fact that they are content with who they are and what they have. This contentment or sense of continuity is reflected in many other aspects of their lives. This trait seems to carry over into their families. Most of them are still married to their original spouses. Divorce has occurred very rarely in this group. To the best of my knowledge, there have been only two divorces among major members of the group. One can argue that this confirms the group's commitment to their loved ones and a continuous awareness of every factor that led to their success.

Another area of interest concerns children following parents into the business. Earlier, I noted several situations where a member of the New Guard succeeded a member of the Old Guard into business. With a few exceptions, most offspring of the mega-millionaires do not follow in their parent's footsteps. One exception is the Werner family, who own Werner Enterprises, the nation's third largest trucking company. The company has reached its current position through its very clever use of technology that allows them to track every move of their trucks. The senior Werner now has all three of his sons playing major management roles in the company he founded. Another exception is Nebraska Furniture Mart and the Blumkin family, described earlier.

Mrs. B has been succeeded by a son-in-law and several grandchildren in the operation of the large furniture store.

For at least a decade, the market has speculated about the fate of Berkshire Hathaway stock when Warren passes to that great boardroom in the sky. During that period, Warren has been mum on the issue, saying little beyond the fact that he has a successor in mind. In early 2000, internet rumors surfaced that Buffett had been ill. Shares of Berkshire dropped steadily until, in very uncharacteristic fashion, the company issued a press release denying the speculation.

Throughout the summer, Buffett reflected on his legacy and in October of 2000, he announced his succession plans. For the purpose of our discussion here, who he will choose to oversee the investments is not as important as who he has chosen as chairman and overseer. His younger son, Howard, will chair the Board of Directors because his father feels that he is best suited to maintain Berkshire's distinct corporate personality. More importantly, this would ensure that the headquarters of Berkshire Hathaway would remain in Omaha.

Another revealing attribute of the Omaha mega-millionaires lies in how they feel about their work and making money. Most people, if asked what they would do if they won the lottery, would probably tell you that the first thing they would do is quit their job. In contrast, those who own and create companies and their attendant wealth appear to believe that it's more fun to make it than to spend it – and they'll keep making it as long as they can. As we pointed out, Mrs. B, Omaha's matriarch mega-millionaire worked until she was 103. Warren Buffett is still active at 70 and talks about running Berkshire Hathaway from the grave via séances. Walter Scott had an opportunity to retire, but instead chose to start a new company.

At one point, Chuck Durham had an opportunity to put a sum of money into the Buffett partnership. Had he done this, he could have an enormous sum of money today as a result of little effort on his part. Instead, he chose to leave the money in his company HDR and put forth his own effort for 30 years. I asked him, "If you had the chance to do it all over again, would you have given the money to Buffett?" He replied, "Probably not!"

To many of them, business is like a game. The way you keep track of how well you are playing is in the amount of money you have. I have often heard them use sports or game metaphors to describe their business like " hitting a homerun" or "using their pawn to capture a fellow business's king. "

To a significant number, this wealth seems to be an object distant from them and not directly connected to them. During the time I spent talking to members of this group, it struck me how they tended to refer to their wealth in the third person. The sense you often get is that it exists beyond them as a kind of abstraction. They know it's there, but they can't really touch it.

Another consequence of this group's work ethic is their tendency to not pass their entire wealth along to their offspring. The prevalent attitude is that passing all their money on to their kids would make the kids lazy at the expense of their self-reliance. As the wealthy grow older, the big question seems to be what to do with their money when they die. Few have plans to spend it all. Foundations and trusts, gifts and donations to local charities and churches have become a major topic of discussion among the older generation of Omaha millionaires. I will have more to say about this later.

To summarize what I have developed so far: The Omaha mega-millionaires made their millions through the ownership of companies that produce very basic goods and services. They love their work, and making millions. They do not view their entrepreneurial efforts as jobs, but as their way of life. They seldom, if ever, really retire. They are not inventors for the most part, and they create nothing new. They made their fortunes by doing ordinary things extraordinarily well. In addition, they keep and expand their wealth by not spending lavishly. Much of their net worth is tied up in investments, leaving them a generous, but not huge, personal income. They have stable families, live simple lifestyles, and when they are old, they are still fabulously wealthy. At that point they consider what to do with some of that wealth, much of which may end up invested in nonprofit foundations and other charitable interests, providing a legacy to benefit their communities.

CHAPTER 9: LIFESTYLES

Let's take a closer look at the lifestyles of these individuals. There are enough commonalities among them to lead one to believe that the way these individuals choose to live is directly correlated to the fact that they have amassed huge amounts of wealth. The homes of the Omaha mega-millionaires reveal a great deal about them. What is most revealing is that the majority of these homes are comfortable and spacious, but no one would call them mansions or estates. Most people tend to think of the very wealthy as either living in a multimillion dollar penthouse on Park Avenue or an estate comparable to the Kennedys' compound in Hyannis.

Chuck Durham's home is typical of some of the homes in this group, a modest house located west of 72nd and south of Pacific, close to the geographical center of Omaha. It is located in an older, established neighborhood where the houses probably contain anywhere from 2,000 to 4,800 square feet. A typical home in this area probably sells for $185,000 to possibly $600,000. The lots are modest and in keeping with the house size. This neighborhood has experienced a phenomenon that is relatively new to Omaha. People are buying $200,000 homes, tearing them down and building $800,000 homes on the lot. But to the best of my knowledge, none of the mega-millionaires have participated in this phenomenon.

According to Chuck, "We built this house in 1945 and moved in

1946. We added on a number of times and did some rebuilding. Everything here has been built and rebuilt and lived in for over 50 years. Ours was one of the first in the neighborhood."

In addition to the living room and family room, there is a dining room that seats 12 and a second dining room near the kitchen with room for eight. There is a large closet off the master bedroom, which Chuck calls his office, where he has a chair and a phone and a television. While these living conditions could not be considered spartan, the Durhams and others like them live well within their means and well below what the average person might assume.

Likewise, Leland Olson, one of the earlier Buffett partners, owns a home about 2-1/2 miles from the Durhams. Leland and his wife built the house in 1954 and have lived in it ever since. It, too, is in a modest neighborhood. I would guess that few of his neighbors are aware of Leland's financial status. Leland does have an office that is bigger than Chuck's. It is probably 8 x 10 feet, with a pleasant view of the backyard. The walls and surfaces are covered with car memorabilia.

Walter Scott's residence is unusual even among this group. He lives in an apartment on an upper floor of the building that houses Peter Kiewit Sons', Inc. in midtown Omaha. Although it is spacious by Omaha standards, it is still modest when compared to penthouse apartments on either of the coasts. As a wealthy pooch, the Scott family pet rides downstairs in the elevator to be taken outside by building security. He has a small dog run in a courtyard area near the building. This may provide the only clue that someone very well to do lives in the building.

Not only do Omaha's wealthy tend to live in homes that are modest relative to their assets, but many of them bought a house at the beginning

Scott's Dog Walk

of their career and continue to live in it today. It is not the least bit unusual to find an Omaha mega-millionaire living in the house they bought when they were just starting out. Many people know that Warren Buffett, the second wealthiest man in America, lives in a two-story bungalow he bought in 1956. What they do not know is that for the Midwest, and particularly for Omaha, Buffett's modest lifestyle is not unusual for this group of mega-millionaires. Warren paid $31,000 for it and it is carried on the Douglas county tax role at $345,000. The only thing that is particularly unusual about the house is that it has a full size handball court in the basement.

In contrast, if you pass through Omaha, you will see some substantial homes on the western edge of town, some which run in the $1 - $3 million range. The best estimate that my real estate experts have on the number of million dollar homes in Omaha is about 100. People tell me that the rich must live there. They may be rich by some standards, but they are not in the mega-millionaires' league. Most of the owners have a couple of things in common. They have significant incomes, which means that somewhere out there is a lender who is dying to provide them with a significant mortgage. Many are what I call "see through" homes. If you go up to the front window, you can see all the way to the back. After they pay their mortgage they don't have any money left over for furniture and drapes.

The point I would like to make here is the relationship of the owner's net worth to the price of the house. Just to make a comparison, one of the ultimate robber barons of the 19th century, Cornelius Vanderbilt built a home that represented 1/2 of 1% of the Gross National Product of the United States. Many members of the New Guard live in a house that is comfortable but represents only about 1/10 of 1% of their net worth. These very wealthy people live well within their means, something many seemingly wealthy people do not do. There are exceptions, but one of the more impressive features of Omaha's wealthy is that they seldom flaunt it.

One notable exception is Joe Ricketts, the head of the on-line brokerage firm, AmeriTrade. In early 1999, Ricketts decided to present his wife, Marlene, with a little surprise. He learned that James Q. Crowe, chief executive officer of the start-up communications company, Level 3, was relocating the company headquarters to Denver. Thus, the Crowe's impressive house would be on the market.

The Crowe home is located very close to the geographical center of Omaha. It is an older section of town populated by mostly up-scale homes. The average sale price for homes in the area is in the $400,000 to $700,000 range. The Crowes purchased the home in 1993 for $1.146 million and spent the next two years remodeling it. It is a

14-room house with seven bedrooms, 10 bathrooms, a six-car garage and an attached guesthouse. The house has a four-acre lot with an outdoor swimming pool and tennis court.

Joe Ricketts bought the house for $7.5 million, by far the largest amount ever paid for a piece of residential property in Omaha. Now came the moment for Ricketts to reveal his surprise. Several of the neighborhood residents told me that his wife, Marlene, had an even bigger surprise for Joe. She refused to live in it. One year later, the gate is locked and the lights are dim. In some ways, Ricketts fits the stereotype that most people have of the very wealthy.

The Runzheimer International Institute, a travel consulting firm, reports that 63% of the nation's top executives have a limousine and a driver. Omaha serves as headquarters for four Fortune 500 companies and I will be darned if I can find their limousines. The only limousines in town that I know of are used for funerals, weddings, and prom nights. Most of the Omaha multi-millionaires drive themselves about town. George Bush came to Omaha during his presidency and drove about town in a limousine. It was obvious he was from out of town.

Many think that the Omaha multi-millionaires drive themselves because they are cheap. But I think they do it because they are too independent to rely on a driver being at the right place at the right time. They would rather not depend on others for their personal needs.

Most people think that the rich drive Rolls Royces or some other expensive or exotic car. Tom Stanley, author of *The Millionaire Next Door*, maintains that the average millionaire drives an older American-made car. Most of Omaha's millionaires drive modest luxury cars such as a Lincoln or Lexus. My best guess is that there are about 24 Rolls Royces in Omaha and probably a similar number of Ferraris, but collectors and car enthusiasts own the majority of them. Dr. Ed James, a member of the Buffett Mdee group, owns two of the Rolls Royces and three of the Ferraris. The Rolls are 1923 and 1924 models, and are not, for obvious reasons, driven daily. They have been entered in numerous vintage auto events, but most of their days are spent under cover in a warm garage. The Ferraris lead a similar existence and my understanding is that they are strictly for investment purposes. There have been some exotic cars purchased by members of the mega-millionaires group, but they are the exception rather than the rule, and they were purchased for the purpose of collecting, not as symbols to make their wealth known to the greater community.

A recent experience of mine further illustrates how this group feels about automobiles, and how they choose to live their lives. Recently, my wife and I were invited to a dinner to celebrate the opening of the Kiewit Institute of Information Technology and Engineering at the University of Nebraska at Omaha.

The event was held at a museum about 20 minutes south of Omaha that houses many of the planes that were used by the Strategic Air Command. There were approximately 1,100 invited guests, including many of Omaha's Old Guard and a considerable number of the New Guard. Both of these groups had contributed very substantial sums of money to the development and ongoing operation of the Peter Kiewit Institute. In short, most of Omaha's wealthy were there that night.

My wife and I pulled up in the rather large parking lot and noticed that approximately a quarter of the lot was roped off and designated as valet parking. We parked approximately a third of the parking lot away from the main entrance, as cars were arriving and the lot was beginning to fill up. As we pulled in and parked, David Sokol, one of the members of the New Guard, pulled up in his Chevy Suburban and parked next to us. Walking into the event, we passed a dozen young men who were serving as the valet parking people. There they were, 11 of the 12 young men, standing around looking at each other in the fairly empty valet lot.

When the evening wrapped up, my wife and I got in our car and headed out of the parking lot. As we were two-thirds of the way out of the lot, we made a right turn to access the road leaving the area. I looked up and saw Warren Buffett and his companion walking over to his car. When I looked over to my left, at the corner of the lot I saw Buffett's eight-year old Lincoln Town Car, which he had parked himself.

Walter Scott drives a Mercedes, but not necessarily a new one. One that he hoped to sell many years ago was an early 1980's Mercedes sedan with well over 100,000 miles on the odometer. Walter allowed an employee to take the car home for the weekend, in order to decide if he wanted to buy it, but the deal fell through because the employee's wife didn't like the ride.

Dr. Leland Olson owns a brand new red Corvette, but the good Doctor is eighty years old. And, in his words "If it's not red, it's not a Corvette." However, he also drives a Dodge pickup truck that is over 12 years old.

When it comes to cars and houses, the Omaha group tends to run counter to the stereotype of the ultra rich, and most of their holdings are modest relative to their net worth. But they are also practical and value their time, so when it comes to corporate jets, they generally make use of them. However, corporate jets are usually owned by the company and are not a personal asset, so various members of the company's leadership may make use of them. And, of course, if you can afford to avoid crowded commercial flights with their delays and other problems, who wouldn't do so?

Todd Duncan, whose family owns Duncan Aviation, a firm that refits and refurbishes corporate jets, says there are 11,656 corporate jets currently registered in the United States. As of this writing, Kansas City has 53 registered jets, Oklahoma City has 68, and Omaha has 53.

One of the first of this group to become involved in corporate aviation was Chuck Durham. Even before his company, HDR, began building its corporate fleet, he had a fancy for flight. He received his pilot's license in 1954 and has logged over 3,000 hours, including 600 in the right seat of a Lear jet. His passion for aviation led to a leadership role in the creation of an aviation program at the University of Nebraska at Omaha. This program includes courses in aeronautical engineering and others related to pilot training..

The most publicized jet in the fleet was the "Indefensible" owned by Berkshire Hathaway and used by the nation's second richest person, Warren Buffett. In January of 1999, the plane flew off to New Jersey to be sold. But Buffett has not headed back to the terminal to stand in line and throw his carry-on in the overhead. He now uses a "time share" jet that he leases through Executive Jet. Executive Jet allows an individual to buy a specified number of flight hours per year. Thus they only pay for what they use which is a very cost-effective means of executive travel. The concept obviously has not eluded Mr. Buffett because he bought the company in 1998.

Those who own or whose companies own jets are not very conspicuous in the community. The jets are parked on the opposite side of the runway from the scheduled passenger terminals in plain hangars. It is very difficult to tell who is in them, since very few of them display corporate logos. Their existence is not a secret, but it is not publicized, either.

One exception is Phil Schrager, who owns Omaha's Pacesetter Corporation, a manufacturer of windows and doors. The company has a corporate jet, which Phil likes to have painted in bright color schemes in keeping with his love for modern art. He tires easily of the paint scheme and likes to repaint periodically.

I have had an opportunity to visit with the pilots who fly the Omaha fleet. It is quite interesting to note that many of the planes that comprise the fleet are not the latest and greatest, top of the line, state-of-the-art aircraft. Many of them were purchased used. The first jet that Berkshire Hathaway owned was twenty years old at the time of purchase. This is the Lear jet equivalent of a '57 Chevy. The plane had a number of maintenance issues and was replaced with a newer used jet after three years. In sum, while the corporate leaders in Omaha are not above making use of the convenience of the corporate jet, they do not flaunt it, and are economical even here.

Private Jet Hanger

The fact that Omaha's mega-millionaires do not lead lavish, ostentatious lifestyles is a fact that should not be taken lightly. It serves to illustrate two very important themes in the lives of these individuals.

They believe in the power of maintaining a humble image, one that does not suggest conspicuous consumption or unnecessary excess. In many ways, their choices serve as a reminder that the amassment of wealth is not about the creation of extravagant lifestyles, but rather, it is about the passion for work and a commitment to the community in which they thrive.

Gorat's – Steakhouse frequented by Omaha's financial elite.

CHAPTER 9

CHAPTER 10: WHY OMAHA?

My belief that the financial/business community of Omaha is uncommonly good at producing wealth should be apparent by now. We have examined who the mega-millionaires are and have identified a number of their common characteristics. Let us now turn our attention to Omaha and the ways in which the city itself factors into this phenomenon of wealth. By now you may be asking, is there something in the nature of the local economy or social structure that led to this? Or is this success story solely attributed to the individuals who created it, regardless of the geographical location? If I can show you why this happened in Omaha, we will better understand the factors that might enable this phenomenon to occur elsewhere.

Why did this occur in Omaha? The first part of the answer is very easy. Most of the Omaha mega-millionaires were born here. While not all of them claim Omaha as the city of their birth, a large majority of them do. Most of the individuals who weren't born in Omaha moved here during their childhood or youth. For example, Rose Blumkin, a Russian immigrant, and Vinod Gupta, from India, came here in their youth. But they made Omaha their home.

Other non-Omaha natives come from assorted less exotic sites. Chuck Durham, founder of engineering firm HDR, was born in Chicago and spent his youth in Ames, Iowa. He then moved to Omaha after graduation from Iowa State University.

The majority of the group not born in Omaha moved here before reaching adulthood. The two most notable exceptions are Ken Stinson and Mike Harper. Stinson, who heads Peter Kiewit Sons', Inc., was born in San Francisco. Harper, who was hired away from General Mills to head the Fortune 500-food giant ConAgra, is from Michigan. Mike Simmonds, our fast food king, is a California native.

Once they arrived in Omaha, they chose to stay because Nebraska's pro business climate made sound economic sense for any type of business. Chuck Durham once went to Chile seeking new business. "Finally, it dawned on me," he said. "Chile's economy is not as big as Nebraska's. If I were back home, I could walk up to City Hall and know everybody there."

As many of them have pointed out to me, Omaha has few distractions. Life in Omaha is just plain easier than it is in many cities. A twenty-mile car ride will provide access to everything in town. My experience is that rush hour in Omaha is less crowded than San Francisco at 2:00 a.m. Stores are plentiful and I have never experienced a pushing and shoving crowd in Omaha like I found at Bloomingdale's at Christmas. Restaurants are plentiful and the cuisine varied, although steak is the dominant menu item. As measured against both Coasts, prices are quite affordable.

Omaha has laid claim to the title, Cultural Center of the Plains. It has 24 live theaters, a professional symphony, an opera company, and a ballet troupe. There is a children's theater, a children's museum, and a youth orchestra. Our art museum, the Joslyn, recently completed a $45 million renovation and expansion program. The zoo, called the Henry Doorly Zoo, has an international reputation. It contains an indoor rainforest and a walk through shark aquarium that is second to none.

The economy here is robust. For the past several decades, Omaha has experienced one of the lowest unemployment rates in the nation. Omaha is known as a recession-proof city because its economic base is so diverse. Its strengths have resulted in a cost of living that is among the lowest in the country.

AK-SAR-BEN

Because of the size of Omaha and the closeness of its business people, a social institution developed which probably could not have grown and flourished in any other town. Named Ak-Sar-Ben, which is Nebraska spelled backwards, this institution not only grew and flourished in Omaha, but it played a major role in the development of the mega-millionaire population.

This club or society, formally called the Knights of Ak-Sar-Ben, was established in 1895 to weld the business and professional men of Omaha into a unified organization that would serve to promote the business interests of the area. Its initial activity was to run the state fair for the state of Nebraska during a period when the state was undergoing significant economic stress due to a downturn in the farm economy.

Over the first half of the 19th century, Ak-Sar-Ben evolved into something of a service or community organization. Its members became involved in fundraising and civic service projects, but it was more than a booster club. Early on, they purchased a racetrack that provided them with a physical center and a ready source of funds.

An integral part of the Ak-Sar-Ben organization has been a festival ball that served as a symbolic harvest celebration. The festival evolved into what is now known as the Coronation Ball, a social event at which a king and a queen of the imaginary land of Quivera are crowned. Being chosen king and queen is a social honor. The criteria for selecting the king and queen are based on their contributions to the community and, to a certain degree, on social pecking order. The king is always socially prominent and the queen is a daughter from an equally prominent Omaha family. Numerous other Omaha families members also participate in the court.

The coronation ball features an elaborate set that supposedly depicts the ancient kingdom of Quivera. The queen wears a modern ball gown, and the king's attire is a traditional costume with a robe and knee britches, long socks, shoes with big buckles, and of course a crown. The *Omaha World-Herald* (Omaha's only daily paper) always publishes a multi-page article on the participants and their backgrounds.

A private Board of Governors directs the organization. The non-paid governors have traditionally been local businessmen who either own a fairly significant company or had an executive position that allowed them the time and expertise to run the organization. The position also requires a significant financial commitment.

The Board of Governors met on a regular basis to conduct the business of the organization. More significantly, it brought together the businessmen of the city on a regular basis and during the Ak-Sar-Ben meetings, they got to know each other. These meetings gave them an opportunity to share business experiences and philosophies. The informal organization created an environment where social values could be shaped and focused. An examination of the membership of the Board of Governors over the past fifty years will reveal the names of many of the Old Guard. Two notable exceptions who have never served on the Board of Governors are Warren Buffett from Berkshire Hathaway and John Lauritzen from First National Bank.

Citizens of Omaha are well aware that they are often viewed as square or unsophisticated by the rest of the nation. But in a very real sense, they don't care. An event that occurred in the 1920s illustrates this. The coronation ball did not yet exist, but by the 1920s, the annual fall harvest festival included a men-only stage show. (Up until the 1930s there were two versions of the show. One for men only and one deemed fit for women to see.)

In 1924 a woman disguised herself as a man and was able to make her way into the men-only show. The next day she told her story, which described the show in detail. Far from being upset or scandalized by what she had seen, it was her conclusion that it was the safest place in Omaha to send a husband.

The name of the show was *Bullfornia*. Frank Latinjer and Gus Renze wrote it. Renze owned a local sign painting and promotional marketing company, which operates today as a trade-show materials production company. *Bullfornia* centered on the character of Richard Cornhusker. (The name has a great deal of significance because the nickname for the University of Nebraska at Lincoln is "The Cornhuskers.")

In the show, Richard Cornhusker dreams of moving to the sunshine state of California. In a short time, he is able to attain incredible wealth and success by investing in oranges and oil wells. As his success, fame, and fortune grow, he enters politics and becomes a well-known local figure.

As the dream continues, he is carried away by this life of fame and fortune and in the process succumbs to the charms of a number of bathing beauties. This leads to his downfall and in a very short period of time he finds himself completely bankrupt. At this point, Richard Cornhusker awakens from his dream and realizes that there's no place like good old Nebraska and he returns to Nebraska and his father's business and spends the rest of his life as a solid, hard-working wage earner.

For some reason, the plot and its thinly veiled title got the attention of a number of national newspapers. California was neither flattered nor excited about the nature of the play and there were several California business organizations that threatened to file a $200,000 damage suit against the authors of the show. The suit never came to fruition, but the publicity was quite extensive and attracted 16,000 men to see the play – 9,000 of whom were out-of-state visitors drawn by the scandalous nature of the show.

I think it is fairly obvious that the notion and nature of *Bullfornia* was not just an isolated figment of the imagination of its two gentlemen authors. In all probability, it spoke to a theme or value that was fairly prevalent among the members of the Omaha community who would also have been members of Ak-Sar-Ben. They were proud of their Midwestern values and not ashamed to be considered hicks by the coastal sophisticates. That is still largely true today. They don't mind being thought of as simple and corny. The innocents of Omaha can laugh all the way to the bank.

Which leads us back to the chicken-egg question. Did they become millionaires because of the city, or did the city become what it is because of them? I think the truth lies in some combination of the above. A unique combination of like-thinking and like-motivated people came together and worked in an environment that supported their success. They are the types of people who would be successful wherever they lived, but being together in one location provided synergies that helped them prosper.

CHAPTER 10

BUFFETT

The outside world and the financial media in particular, view Omaha as Warren Buffett's fiefdom. To them, he put Omaha on the financial map. Many eyes focusing on Omaha could only see Buffett. The accumulation of personal wealth in Omaha has been attributed to Buffett by many of the financial media. Without him, there would be no Omaha Buffett-style mega-millionaires.

But what about the influence Omaha has had on Buffett and the contribution it made in molding his philosophy and value system? He attended local public schools in Omaha and graduated from the University of Nebraska. He played with kids from Omaha and listened to them during the years when his values and personality were being formed. Following his graduation from Columbia University, he sought employment in New York. It didn't work out and he returned to Omaha to start the Buffett Partnership. This would later become Berkshire Hathaway.

Many Omaha residents can recall the sight of a crew cut, 20-year-old Buffett canvassing the community seeking enough investment capital to launch his career. Not only was he asking investors for $10,000, which at the time represented a very substantial amount of money, he had no track record, would not tell them what he was investing in, and proposed to keep 25% of the profits above 6%.

If he had lived in the Big Apple and made his solicitations there, would he have raised enough money? Obviously, we will never have the definitive answer to that question, but I do think it is safe to say that he would have found a much less sympathetic market. No matter how talented they are, no money manager will ever get anywhere without any money to manage.

Granted, there were a significant number of "non-Omaha" residents among the original Buffett partners. But an examination of when they entered in the timeline is telling. First came family members, then neighbors, and then friends. The out-of-towners did not begin to enter the partnership until he had established a bit of a track record and the word of mouth had a chance to spread.

Not only did Omaha provide Buffett with the investors willing and able to invest on his terms, but they also possessed the unique approach to life and investing necessary to make the whole thing work. To amass the size of fortunes they have, it required investors who would not bolt from the fold at the first sign of trouble in the market. They also had to be steadfast enough not to take the tremendous gains that the investment produced over time and, on a whim, turn it into a new house, boat or other toy. I am not suggesting that he would have never found these types of investors elsewhere, but Omaha provided them in bulk.

Omaha also provided Buffett with an environment in which he could think clearly and that was free from distraction. He has spoken of the din of the crowd on Wall Street, one that could force you to take your eye off the ball. His approach to business requires singularity of thinking that can't be led astray when the news of the day intervenes. Omaha provided him with a comfortable place to escape and be allowed to rely on his own devices.

Omaha also provided him with his Vice Chairman and alter ego, Charlie Munger, along with his first outside Director, Walter Scott. These two men played significant roles in the path that Berkshire has taken. Without them, Berkshire Hathaway would look a lot different that it does today. Munger's participation in the day-to-day operation of Berkshire has been on the wane for several years, but there can be no doubt that he played a pivotal role in the development of Berkshire's investment philosophy in the years after the partnership evolved. So, while Buffett played a role in the creation of the financial market in Omaha, I think it is also safe to say that Omaha played a role in the creation of the icon that is Warren Buffett.

A POWERFUL NETWORK

In the years during which the Old Guard was developing, there existed a more tightly-knit social group than you would have found in many other communities. Because of that, such critical elements as cultural values and other crucial attitudes that are passed on and shared are transmitted in a far easier fashion. They include such cultural values as the belief that one's destiny can be influenced through their own considerable action. There is a high level of value placed upon working, achieving and saving, and disdain placed upon the flaunting of one's wealth and conspicuous consumption.

Towards the end of World War II when the Old Guard was putting down their economic and business roots, there were two individuals in the community who were highly visible to the other members of the group. They were Peter Kiewit, Jr. and V.J. Skutt, the President and Chairman of the Board of Mutual of Omaha. Mutual of Omaha was and still is, as its name implies, a mutually owned company. It is owned by the policyholders of the company. It does not have individuals who have equity participation as you do with a privately held company or a publicly traded company. Mutual of Omaha has been in Omaha since the late 20s and continues to be a major employer. It's interesting that it does not play the same role in the generation of individual wealth that any of these other companies play, simply because of the corporate structure and nature of the ownership of the company. While there have been a large number of people who have worked for the company and have made a comfortable living, they never accumulated the large net worth we are talking about.

Kiewit and Skutt both shared some very strong and dominant personality characteristics. Although I never had the opportunity to meet either one, descriptions by their peers and contemporaries provide that both men were very hard working, dedicated people. They were the kind of people you would turn to when you wanted something done. These two men were the center of much of the business activity and very involved with Ak-Sar-Ben. They were highly visible. They were admired for their successes and they served as very strong role models, particularly during the development of the Old Guard.

Peter Kiewit's example and most of his money continues to have an impact on Omaha today. He had an incredible work ethic, insisting that the job be done and be done right. He not only preached it, but he lived it. He believed that in order to work the kind of hours needed for the company's

CHAPTER 10

success, his employees needed to be healthy. So he gave his employees the time and the equipment to exercise their bodies – as well as their minds.

The Old Guard spent time together, thus allowing them to get to know one another and to share their social, political, and business philosophies. It is impossible to know whether they developed their social and business values independently or as a collective group, but one can be fairly certain that the involvement of these individuals with one another served to clarify and reinforce a common set of values. As these relationships grew and developed, similarities between their companies became more and more apparent. They exchanged ideas and information. It wasn't long before they began to play integral roles in each other's companies.

It was during this period that Omaha's major food processing company, ConAgra, began to experience financial problems that stemmed primarily from their operations in Puerto Rico. The Board of Directors sought outside help to replace the existing CEO, Allan Mactier. They turned to the head of a farm products manufacturer, Valmont Industries, for support. Bob Daugherty, the head of Valmont, helped them recruit Mike Harper from Pillsbury and later, placed Mike on Valmont's Board.

The Old Guard continued to crossover among the Boards of various Omaha companies. This practice continues today as individuals such as Walter Scott, Bob Daugherty, Bruce Rohde, Ken Stinson, etc., sit on many of the Boards of Old Guard companies.

IT MUST BE THE WATER

Let's turn our attention to a microcosm of Omaha wealth – Kiewit Plaza. It would be safe to say that the Kiewit Plaza has seen the creation of somewhere in the neighborhood of four or five billionaires and perhaps several hundred multi-millionaires. The Kiewit Plaza itself is a nondescript, rather plain looking building with an austere, beige facade, built in what used to be the middle of Omaha, but now would be considered the eastern edge of town. It is a 15-story building with about 150,000 square feet of rather sterile-looking office space.

Around 1959, Peter Kiewit and Chuck Durham were having lunch. In the course of discussion, they both agreed that their firms had outgrown their current office space and could use some new office space. Here you have the head of a construction firm, one of the country's largest in terms of projects, and the head of an architectural/engineering design firm. The two of them got together and went looking for a sight.

Kiewit Plaza

CHAPTER 10

After several months, they determined that a site at 36th and Farnam was adequate in terms of size and proximity to the rest of town. Durham's firm, HDR, went to work, completed the design drawings and then Peter Kiewit Sons', Inc. went to work on the actual project. During the project, Peter Kiewit, who was an almost constant presence on the site, decided that since they were going to such great lengths, effort, and expense to build this building, he wanted it to include a private dinner club and apartments on the upper floors.

During the construction phase, the head of Bozell & Jacobs, one of the larger advertising firms in the country and Omaha's largest local firm at the time, approached Durham and Kiewit and said that they too needed additional office space and that if there was any room in the plaza, they would like to participate. The history of the building becomes more interesting, less from an architectural and engineering perspective, and more from a financial and business perspective.

Approximately four years after completion, the engineering firm HDR continued to expand its business and decided it was time for them to seek new space because Kiewit was growing at the same time. HDR did move out of the building and built a new office complex for themselves farther out west along the main east-west corridor of Omaha, on Dodge Street. Durham himself went on to become a multi-multi-millionaire and in the early 70s the firm was bought by a French concern. In the process, most of the principals of the firm walked away from HDR with many, many, millions of dollars.

About the same time that HDR was leaving, Warren Buffett's operation had gone from the limited partnership mentioned earlier to become Berkshire Hathaway. Buffett determined at that time that it was no longer prudent to be operating out of the sunroom in his home and moved into a small 500-square-foot area of the Kiewit Plaza on the 14th floor. The rest, as they say, is history.

The last and possibly the largest success story at 36th & Farnam has been that of Peter Kiewit Sons', Inc. The employee-owned company has become very successful because of its aggressive business stance and commitment to hard work and effort. Consequently, there are many Kiewit employees who are millionaires, ranging anywhere from several million dollars to tens of millions. But some of this wealth was the result of the involvement of Peter Kiewit Sons', Inc. in outside business operations, not via their ownership of company stock. As you can see, the Kiewit Plaza has played a very major role in millionaire production-so much so that at one point *Forbes* wrote an article about the building called, "It Must Be the Water." The Kiewit story is a prime example of how the efforts and partnership atmosphere of the Omaha business community resulted in great success for its members.

LOCATION, LOCATION

As previously mentioned, the wealth amassed by the Omaha mega-millionaires resulted from the ownership of companies. There were several aspects of the Omaha cultural and physical environment that put constraints on the types of business they were able to develop. Nature also played a major role in determining the direction the companies of the Omaha millionaires would take. Beginning with the Old Guard, Omaha and the surrounding area had no major natural resources that could be used as raw material for the production of anything. There are no oil fields, no gold mines, no coalmines, no major forests or any thing of this nature located in Nebraska. Thus, any product manufactured here would require the raw material to be transported in from the outside.

Which leads us to our second point. Omaha is located in the geographical center of the United States. Years ago, any goods that it produced would have a fairly high transportation cost for both the raw materials and final product, which would of course increase the cost of production. If major manufacturing activities were to develop in Nebraska, they would require that the raw material be shipped to Omaha, then the product manufactured and shipped back to the consumer – putting the city at an economic disadvantage.

Another feature of Omaha, which played a role in the type of businesses that were developed, was the fact that Omaha lacked a major technical or research university. If Omaha was to have companies that developed new products and technologies in either the electronic or medical fields, it would not have the research center and personnel to support it.

There are a number of studies to support the contention that Nebraska is lagging behind other states in terms of their participation in the new high-tech economy. One of these studies was conducted in the summer of 1999 by a think-tank group affiliated with the Democratic Leadership Council. It was a study that ranked all of the states in descending order and the rankings were based on 17 measures including education of the states workforce and presence on the internet. Currently, Nebraska ranks 36th in terms of its high-tech economic base. Massachusetts, California, and Colorado are at the head of the group. At the back of the group are West Virginia, Arkansas, and Mississippi.

To further elaborate on the results of the study, some of the areas in which the state fell down was in commercial internet domain names, where Omaha ranks 20th. In terms of scientists and engineers as a percentage of the workforce, it was 34th. In industrial investment and research in development as a share of gross domestic state product, Omaha ranked 41st and in venture capital invested as a percentage of state gross domestic product we were 42nd. Several areas which point to a brighter future include the technology in schools. In a weighted measure of the percentage of classrooms wired for Internet, teachers with technology training in schools with more than 50% of the teachers having school based e-mail accounts, Nebraska ranked 4th in the nation. This is an excellent sign that the upcoming generation is being trained and skills are being generated for the high-tech environment.

All of this applies to the Old Guard. Many of the factors which determine the nature of the Old Guard companies have actually worked in favor of the companies of the New Guard. The New Guard is heavily involved in telecommunication, electronic banking, and electronic brokerage. In these businesses, Omaha's location and environment have proven to be a strong plus.

Take, for example, the telecommunications business. Obviously, in regard to telecommunications, location plays a significantly different role than it does in manufacturing. Couple this with the fact that during the Cold War, the headquarters of the Strategic Air Command was located on a base on the southeast fringe of Omaha. The nature of the Strategic Command as it developed during the Korean War through the Vietnam War and into the mid-1980's was such that it required major cable/ground/telephone/communication. The nature of this business is such that location is irrelevant, as long as the product can be delivered via the telephone lines and increasingly over the airwaves. Another element of this whole scenario lies in the fact that since Omaha is in the middle of the country, its citizens lack a discernible accent, allowing companies to better communicate and be understood in all parts of the country.

So, have I answered the "Why Omaha?" question? Not definitively, but I hope I have identified many contributing factors. A number of strong, unique role models who were instrumental in developing a community value system; a unique institution in Ak-Sar-Ben, and an environment that forced business in a specific product direction all contributed to the unique economic environment of Omaha and the success of its outstanding players.

CHAPTER 11: GIVING BACK TO THE COMMUNITY

The next decade represents a watershed for both the Omaha business community and the community as a whole as the members of the Old Guard approach the end of their lifespan. What happens to the assets will have a profound impact on the social and economic fabric of the city.

There are two issues in Omaha's succession planning. The first issue revolves around what will happen to the companies, and the second is related to what will become of the accumulated wealth. In the case of the publicly traded companies, succession in the leadership is already taken care of. Most of the companies have managers very much in the mold of the founder. I anticipate that there will be very little if any discernible change in the day-to-day operation of the companies and, little, if any change in the goods they produce.

In the majority of the cases, as noted earlier, the children do not usually follow the parent into the business. One of the exceptions is the First National Bank of Omaha, the largest bank headquartered in Omaha. The Lauritzen family has been involved in the bank for most of the twentieth century and currently holds a majority of the outstanding stock. The banking industry is currently in a phase of merger and consolidation that may continue for another decade. But the Lauritzen family has stated that they have no intention of selling or relinquishing control. Until recently, when failing health caused him to retire, John Lauritzen ran the bank. His son Bruce took control upon his father's departure. A son/grandson of the current management is currently at Goldman Sach's in New York and may be grooming to take the helm when the time comes. A sister, Meg, has been in the business for a number of years.

The other notable exception involves Werner Enterprises, where all three of the founder's sons are involved in the business. Clarence Werner began Werner Enterprises in 1956. In that year he took his life savings and the proceeds from the sale of a pickup truck and purchased the company's first eighteen wheeler. From that humble beginning the company has grown steadily and is now the third largest truckload carrier in the country. The company boasts a fleet of 6,800 semi-trailers with routes and terminals spanning the nation. They are currently in the process of expanding their operations to include Canada and Mexico. One of Clarence's three sons is expected, when the time comes for Clarence to step down, to take the helm.

The rest of the Old Guard companies will experience new management with new last names. Some have already occurred such as Mogens Bay at Valmont, and Ken Stinson at Kiewit.

That loosely sums up the possible directions for the companies, but what about the money? We know that they are not going to spend it all or give it to their kids. Most couldn't spend it all even if they wanted to. The only viable alternative then would be to give it away, either during their lifetime or at their passing.

When I say that the money will not go to the children, this does not mean that there are no provisions for them. Those with children have made it clear that only a small portion of their wealth will pass unencumbered to the next generation. The prevailing attitude is that the money the kids do receive represents a nest egg or starter yeast that they can use to start their own future, that if the kids received enough money for them to live the rest of their lives in luxury, they would lose their incentive. The intention here is to maintain the children's work ethic and initiative, thereby giving them the opportunity to shape their own futures.

The reason most often given by this group for not passing their fortunes to their offspring is that they want their children to grow up to be independent, work for themselves, and develop good habits and skills. There is another contributing factor as well. Most of them maintain the strong belief that they have been blessed by the community and society and that they, in turn, have an obligation to give back to the community most of what they have been given. The method of choice in the vast majority of these situations is that they have established or will establish (most of the Old Guard already has) some sort of charitable foundation.

I had an opportunity to visit with Nick Taylor, an attorney with the Omaha law firm of Fitzgerald, Schorr, Barmettler, & Brennan. Taylor is probably the foremost authority in Omaha on foundations and charitable trusts, and has been involved in the establishment of many of them. He described for me three general categories of charitable giving that encompass most of the Omaha trusts and foundations.

In the first category, the trustees are directed by the donor family or company to direct their giving towards a variety of different activities that will be specifically beneficial to city of Omaha. In terms of dollar amount, I would estimate that this is probably the smallest group of foundations.

The second category of foundation involves giving that's directed towards some specific cause, such as a cure for cancer, population control, or environmental concerns. Again, I would estimate that the amount of money involved here is a little bit larger than that directed specifically at Omaha, but still does not constitute the largest group.

The last type of foundation has no specific design or charter directing the giving. The person or company has established a foundation with a board of directors, but the types of activities or causes to which those dollars will be directed are not specifically described. The ramifications of this are quite far-reaching. On one hand, the amount of money funding this sort of foundation is very large, and some of it could be directed to Omaha. But there's a strong possibility that a very large portion of it may also go to support activities that are literally global in nature.

When you mention "charitable giving" in Omaha, Nebraska, and the impact that it has had on this city, you can't do it without the name "Lied" coming up. You will see a significant number of buildings and institutions with the name on it. For example, at the University of Nebraska Medical Center there's a Lied Transplant Center, at the University of Nebraska in Lincoln, the Lied Center for the Performing Arts, and in Nebraska City, the Lied Conference Center. Lied is a name that is known to most of the Omaha community only in that context.

Ernie Lied was born and raised in Ohio and moved to Omaha later in life. Not much is known about Mr. Lied, who spent most of his life in Las Vegas. Colleagues describe him as a loner. Apparently, at one time, he ran a Buick dealership in Omaha, but in approximately 1956 or 1957, he sold it and moved to Las Vegas, Nevada. When he arrived in Las Vegas he began buying a lot of land. Soon, the money that Ernie had invested into land in Las Vegas became extremely valuable. Lied never married and died relatively young, leaving his money to a foundation administered by his former secretary. Today, the Lied Foundation has grown to quite a sizeable charity and has directed many, many millions of dollars to causes in Omaha and across the Midwest.

There are two basic ways in which the Omaha mega-millionaires are participating in philanthropy in the distribution of their assets. One, of course, is to establish a charitable foundation or trust that makes use of the funds after their death. However, many of the prominent Old Guard members have contributed during their lifetimes, such as Walter Scott, Chuck Durham and Leland Olson. Scott has played a major role in many community initiatives such as the Henry Doorly Zoo, which is one of the world's finest. There are a number of exhibits in the Zoo that bear the names of Walter and Suzanne Scott. One of the more unique exhibits is the new shark aquarium which contains a glass tunnel through which visitors can walk and experience a sense of being in the water with the sharks and other underwater life. It is a stunning experience, to say the least. Walter and Suzanne Scott have also been very generous to the University of Nebraska, and, as noted elsewhere, Walter Scott played a key role in the development of the Peter Kiewit Institute for Information, Science, Technology, and Engineering.

The Lied Foundation donated funds to the Zoo to create an indoor rainforest, the Lied Jungle. It is approximately five stories tall and visitors can walk on a winding walkway above a pond and lake system where numerous birds and mammals, including primates, a dwarf hippopotamus, and even a few crocodiles roam about uncaged.

Chuck Durham and his late wife, Marge, have also been prominent in the community. There is a Boy Scout headquarters that bears the Durham name, as well as the Western Heritage Museum, devoted to local and regional history. Like the others, the Durhams have made a number of contributions to the University as well.

Leland Olson has been most generous with his assets, and as befits his medical background, his primary contributions have been to the University of Nebraska Medical Center. The Olsons prefer not to talk about the amount of their donations, but they have contributed significant amounts to help in the construction of many projects associated with the Lied Transplant Center. They have also endowed a number of programs at the Olson Center for Women's Health, as well as endowing the Chris and Marie Olson Clinical Investigation in Obstetrics and Gynecology, named in honor of Olson's parents.

I have heard some criticism in the community that the younger generation does not appear to be as philanthropic as the older generation. This may be partially due to the simple fact that they are still building up their businesses and are not yet in a position to distribute the proceeds of a lifetime of business success.

Lied Transplant Center

However, there are individuals within the New Guard who give every indication that the Old Guard's legacy of giving back to the community will continue. Notable is Terry Watanabe, owner of the Oriental Trading Company. Watanabe tells the story of a time when he was a very young man and his father gave him some money and instructed him to donate it to causes related to diseases such as cancer, arthritis, etc. So, at a very early age, his father provided for him a role model for inspiration and support.

In June of 2000, Watanabe announced that he had hired a former Time Warner executive by the name of Steven Frary to take over the day-to-day operations of Oriental Trading Company. This would enable Watanabe to devote more of his time to charitable activity.

Watanabe has spent the last 30+ years of his life, ever since his father passed away in 1977, building the business and reports that many times he's working 80, 85 – 95 hours a week. Just recently Watanabe gave $1,000,000 to United Way of the Midlands and has spent the last five years putting together and developing the Terry Watanabe Charitable Trust. He has been candid in pointing out that his plans for his charity and community support are directly related to the success of the business and that the more the business is able to grow, the more he hopes to be able to contribute to the community. In addition, Watanabe has also been a strong supporter of Opera Omaha, the Henry Doorly Zoo, and he plans to continue to support agencies working to help young people.

CHAPTER 11

Another visible member of the New Guard is Vinod (Vinny) Gupta, the Chairman and CEO of *info*USA. Over the past few years, Gupta has been very generous with contributions to the University of Nebraska, but last year, he also donated money for and was very instrumental in the creation of a school in the small city in India where he grew up. In order to get it started, he has donated $1,000,000 of his own money to build the school. Very little has changed in the 40 years since Gupta left the village, and water, electricity, and other resources are still scarce. The school will be named the Shrimati Ram Rati Gupta Women's Polytechnic College after Gupta's late mother. Plans are that approximately 250 women will attend the school, where educational opportunities for women are very few. Gupta's goal is to help break this cycle of poverty, illiteracy, and dependence for women. The ongoing funding of the school will be helped by Gupta's charitable foundation, which is run by his uncle. The hope is that within the next few years, the school will be able to expand to approximately 500 students.

These are just a few of the many individuals who contribute significant resources to charitable efforts. As mentioned earlier, most of the mega-millionaires have established some type of charitable trust or foundation. According to Earl Taylor, who at the time was the Executive Director of the Omaha Community Foundation, all are classified under the Internal Revenue Code as Section 501(c)3 organizations, or nonprofit organizations established for charitable or educational purposes. All (c)3 corporations must file a statement with the government that describes the purpose or mission of the foundation. It's important to recognize that the intent under the law of these foundations is to give at least the income, if not some of the assets, to an organization, group, purpose or cause other than the families of the founders or donors. So these foundations are not set up for the purpose of sheltering any assets against taxes to be passed on to relatives.

According to Earl Taylor, as of August of 1999, there were 536 such organizations in the city of Omaha. There are two ways these organizations can operate: (1) They can be set up and not immediately funded. If the individual or individuals involved are still living, they can take current income or current assets and place it in the foundation to be paid out during that tax year. (2) Upon the death of the individuals involved, the assets so designated by the donor can be placed in the foundation, which is then managed by a Board of Directors which is responsible for the investment of the assets and making grants, or deciding which charities or causes receive financial support from the foundation.

Foundations can either be stand-alone foundations, which have their own individual board of directors, or in many cities, including Omaha, there exists the opportunity to use a larger, umbrella foundation. In Omaha, the Omaha Community Foundation facilitates the charitable giving process and in doing so, seeks to improve the quality of life in Omaha.

The impact these assets could have on Omaha's future is considerable. The best estimate I have of the potential net worth of these foundations is in the $30 billion dollar range. You must understand this is a moving target. Many things could happen between the time this is written and the time the last member of the Buffett group and Old Guard passes on. A number of years with a strong stock market has the potential to double that figure, and a weak market could lessen it. Nonetheless, there is a significant amount of accumulated wealth that has and will continue to support nonprofit causes in the foreseeable future.

I pointed out earlier that very few of the offspring of the Omaha mega-millionaires followed in their parents' footsteps and went into the same business or took over control of the company that the parent had started. However, there are a number of foundations that are being directed by the younger generation of these millionaires.

For example, Warren Buffett's foundation at this time is being headed up by his daughter, Susie, and Walter Scott has given each of his four children a sizeable amount of money to establish foundations under their own auspices.

Because of the success and generosity of this group, Omaha is already a different and better place. Omaha has a first-class zoo, recreational facilities, a world-class teaching/research hospital and soon could have one of the top 10 technical research and teaching facilities.

During the last decade or so, Omaha's University of Nebraska Medical Center has gone from a typical University hospital to a world class research center. Currently, the University of Nebraska Medical Center is recognized both nationally and throughout the world for the research and the applications it has conducted in both cancer research and organ transplantation. As a functioning hospital, the University of Nebraska Medical Center has grown to the point where it no longer serves only patients from the Omaha, Nebraska area. It is not the least bit unusual for patients to come from all parts of the United States for chemotherapy treatment, liver transplants, and various other organ transplants. Patients have come from as far as South America to receive treatment at the Med Center. Among its notable patients is Robert Redford's son who came to Omaha several years ago for an organ transplant. He has been back several times to thank the staff and to help promote the work that is going on there.

The members of the "Old Guard" have played a major role in the growth and recognition of the University of Nebraska Medical Center. A significant amount of public or private money has been donated to the University, often with matching donations either from the public or private sector. Numerous people, including Nancy O'Brien, the chairperson of the Board of Regents of the University of Nebraska system, have told me that had it not been for the donations and supporting efforts of these individuals, the University of Nebraska Medical Center would not have reached the levels that it enjoys today. Prominent among these philanthropists are Chuck Durham and his late wife, Marge, Leland Olson and the Lied Foundation.

   The City of Omaha and the surrounding community have experienced a major change because of the presence of the Omaha mega-millionaires. They had the desire, energy and foresight to apply their wealth toward the creation of a major research university. In addition, they contributed their time, energy, and influence. In the mid 90s, over 250,000 vacant jobs in the technical sector existed. Since 1996, that number has grown to approximately 90,000 vacant jobs per year. Walter Scott recognized that this problem had not only national impact, but it was one that was having a major impact on the city of Omaha and the state of Nebraska. Companies like Peter Kiewit Sons', Inc. and Level 3 Communications were having a difficult time attracting the best trained technical students. In 1996, with a great deal of effort from Walter Scott and Nancy O'Brien of the Board of Regents of the University of Nebraska, the concept of the Peter Kiewit Institute was formed. The Institute was designed to train people in the use of computer technology and its many applications to business, finance, and such professions as engineering. The funding for the physical institute came from what is, in the academic world, a unique combination of both public and private funds. The Peter Kiewit Foundation played a generous part in these activities as did many other corporations and individuals in Nebraska.

   The Peter Kiewit Institute is located on the site of the former Ak-Sar-Ben horse race track. For a major part of the twentieth century, Ak-Sar-Ben funded its activities from the money that was generated by horseracing at the Omaha track. In the mid 80's, a greyhound racing track was built in Council Bluffs, Iowa – Omaha's sister city which is located immediately across the Missouri River from Omaha. It was evident early on that the greyhound activities would begin to have a negative impact on the revenues of the Ak-Sar-Ben horse track. Then, in the early 90s, changes in Iowa gaming laws allowed a number of casinos to be built along the river in Council Bluffs. This further accelerated the erosion of the gambling base that had attracted

Peter Kiewit Institute

horseracing at Ak-Sar-Ben. After few years, live horseracing and the associated gambling virtually disappeared from Omaha.

This left Ak-Sar-Ben with no major source of funding and it also left a rather large tract of land in the middle of Omaha vacant. So, it was on this sight that Walter Scott, in conjunction with the University of Nebraska at Omaha, First Data Resources, the University of Nebraska system and many private citizens and corporations, decided to build the Peter Kiewit Institute.

The student body at the Peter Kiewit Institute is heavily recruited from among the brightest students in the state of Nebraska. Every effort is made by the University and the Institute to not only provide these students with the finest training available but to provide them with the incentives to remain and pursue their careers in Nebraska. Students at the Peter Kiewit Institute learn through a method that is quite different than the conventional university or academic situation.

As many as 150 fully funded Scott Scholars attend UNO and the Institute, living in housing specifically designed for their needs and studying in an environment that is conducive to continual learning. They learn from distinguished faculty from the University, but they also have an opportunity to receive guest lectures and hands-on experience from business leaders and engineering and technical individuals who come from all over the country. Early on in the process, Boeing Corporation became interested in what was going on at the Peter Kiewit Institute and asked the Institute if they could provide a visiting scholar program at the Institute. This would provide students with the opportunity to learn directly from those working in the field.

CHAPTER 11

Another unique facet of the Kiewit Institute's program is in the area of actual hands on application. The building that houses the Institute was constructed with the purpose of providing many different engineering applications and its testing labs are designed to provide the physical means for students to run those hands-on applications. As you can see, the success of the Old Guard, who made their fortunes for the most part in non-technical industries, has ironically provided the funds to give the city the gift of additional technological educational facilities.

This is the end of the book but the beginning of the story. The next decade will reveal how Omaha will change because this group of people lived here and accomplished what they did. Their ambition made them rich, but their generosity and foresight will change the institutions and social fabric in a way that could dramatically alter the business environment. Not only will the face of Omaha change, but the coming decades will see the legacy of the Omaha mega-millionaires alter the world.

CHAPTER 12: CONCLUSION

A careful examination of these individuals seems to suggest that people choose their level of income. Your initial response to this suggestion might be, "If I chose my level of income, I certainly wouldn't have chosen the one I have." As we have seen throughout this book, individuals who amass great amounts of wealth do so by following a particular kind of path. They chose to follow that path. Likewise, many of us choose a certain profession and accept the compensation available for members of that profession.

What is so interesting about the Omaha mega-millionaires is that they come from such different backgrounds and made their millions by providing different products and services, but still there are undeniable similarities in terms of how they went about attaining their wealth.

Mrs. B started one of the largest furniture stores in the country with only $500. Bob Daugherty made the ranks of the mega-millionaires with an investment of his life savings, which was about $5,000. The point I want to make is that these entrepreneurs started with very little and created their wealth from small beginnings. There are many ways that an individual can get the money to begin or buy a company, but without question, a bit of risk is involved. One has to be willing to make sacrifices, if necessary, to build a small nest egg. This might require modifications of one's lifestyle, and many individuals hesitate to make the necessary adjustments that might, in the end, significantly alter their level of wealth. My intention here is to bring the existence of such choices to your conscious awareness. It is there. It's just not something we tend to examine through the lens of personal choice.

We choose our goals. If we choose to save an amount of money sufficient to start a company, we do so at the expense of other choices. When I was teaching economics, one of the concepts that was constantly emphasized is that no decision is a decision. Perhaps you can't decide whether or not to save money for the purpose of investing in a small project or business. By not deciding, you are making a decision. There are many values in life worth pursuing and money is only one of them. But all pursuits require choice, decision, and action.

The pursuit of great wealth also requires risk. But the degree of risk that an individual might be willing to take varies even among the very wealthy. Certain individuals reach a particular goal or comfort level and decide to stop taking additional risks. At a certain level, risk becomes a relative concept. Once a business reaches a particular size, certain risks may impact the business in different ways. For example, opening a new outlet when one already has three hundred outlets, presents a relatively small risk, as its success or failure won't jeopardize the business as a whole. But buying another business or devoting the time and resources necessary to start off in a new direction might put the whole enterprise at risk. Some of the most successful businesses were able to take those large leaps.

My particular assessment of the Omaha mega-millionaires is that they are indeed risk-takers, but they are not thrill seekers or gamblers. This is to say that they not only understand the risks presented to them, but they have a clear understanding of the measures they must take in order to manage those risks.

An appropriate illustration of this phenomenon is Mike Yanney. Mike started buying agriculture-related businesses in the late 1970's in the former USSR. The Soviet Union was just beginning to explore the possibilities of expanded trade with the west, but it was still very much a centrally controlled economy in a Communist nation. A change in the political situation could have resulted in the loss of his investment without much in the way of recourse. This presented a significant risk. Mike Yanney understood all of the ramifications of this situation and was still able to manage the risk through the relationships he had established. There were inherent risks in investing at a time of relative political instability, but there was also the possibility of great rewards. As it worked out, his efforts were well-timed and, in spite of many uncontrollable factors, his investments paid off.

By avoiding risk, you potentially avoid rewards. This certainly explains why owning businesses is one way to achieve wealth. Deciding to be an entrepreneur requires that one take the risks inherent in such a choice. Not everyone is willing to take those risks, but for those who want to know the true secret behind great wealth, I contend that the risk of self-employment and thereby ownership is a large part of the answer.

Another obstacle that tends to keep individuals from attaining the wealth they desire lies in their perceptions about skill. Many people think that they simply don't have the proper training. The impressions I have received throughout the course of my discussions is that many of these wealthy individuals did not enter the business world with the kinds of skills that one might consider necessary. That is to say, they did not train for careers as entrepreneurs. They are skilled in far more important ways. Namely, the desire to make the project work and the willingness to put forth the effort and take the risks required in order to achieve a desired result. There are no schools of entrepreneurship and the backgrounds of most mega-millionaires are diverse. In sum, what these individuals have in common does not boil down to a body of knowledge so much as it does to an attitude. They all had the desire to achieve success, the willingness to take risks, and the ability to stay focused on their goals.

Let us not forget the paradox that is threaded throughout the book: This is not about money. The energy that the mega-millionaires focused on building their business empires is only peripherally about money. At heart, it is about the gamesmanship of making money, and the successful player approaches the game with the following skills:

- Character
- Desire
- Focus
- Perseverance
- Work

The mega-millionaires demonstrate time and again that building significant amounts of assets can be done over time. Over the course of a number of years, focused effort and perseverance pays off. It has nothing to do with the appearance of wealth and the kind of money that parades through the modern media. It is a life's work and passion that creates true wealth.

As we saw in previous chapters, common value systems, the interconnectedness of individuals and companies, and a commitment to the community all play crucial roles in the creation of Omaha's wealth. These companies provide jobs and investment opportunities and the money generated by this group of individuals has impacted the city in a wide variety of positive ways. They teach us that the creation of wealth involves a myriad of personal choices, but it also involves a willingness to participate in the greater community, to pay attention to its history and fabric, and to operate in a way that honors the great game of business.

APPENDIX

After 25 years of experience in the Omaha business community, I have concluded that Omaha's financial picture is unusual because:
1. Omaha has a higher than average concentration of millionaires, particularly *mega-millionaires* whose personal net worth exceeds $100 million.
2. A significant and unusual amount of the wealth created by this group comes from owning publicly traded companies. (This is different than the results of other studies, which generally have concluded that most millionaires were the very frugal owners of small businesses or had exceptionally high incomes. But remember, here we are talking about the mega-millionaire, not the garden-variety millionaire!)
3. The companies owned by Omaha millionaires tend to be companies with simple products, yet with profitability well above the national average.
4. The Omaha business environment is a major factor in a company's success.

We can begin to get a view of the size and nature of the wealth in Omaha by looking at something called *market capitalization.* The market capitalization of a publicly traded company is simply the value of the outstanding shares of stock, or the number of shares multiplied by the market price of the share. The market capitalization of the publicly traded companies headquartered in Omaha exceeds that of Kansas City by about 35%. To put it in perspective for you, Kansas City is approximately 2-1/2 times larger than Omaha in population. Omaha's market cap is 15 times larger than Oklahoma City, whose metropolitan population is 55% larger than Omaha.

Omaha is home to four Fortune 500 companies. These include ConAgra, Berkshire Hathaway, Mutual of Omaha, and Peter Kiewit Sons', Inc. Of the 500 largest corporations in the world, two are headquartered in Omaha. This includes ConAgra, a multi-faceted food conglomerate that, on a revenue basis, is larger than Coca-Cola and Berkshire Hathaway. The index of Nebraska stocks has exceeded both the Dow and the Standard & Poor's 500 for the last eight years. The average rates of return on investment for Omaha companies are almost double that of the national average.

POPULATION STATISTICS
(Source: The 1997 Census)

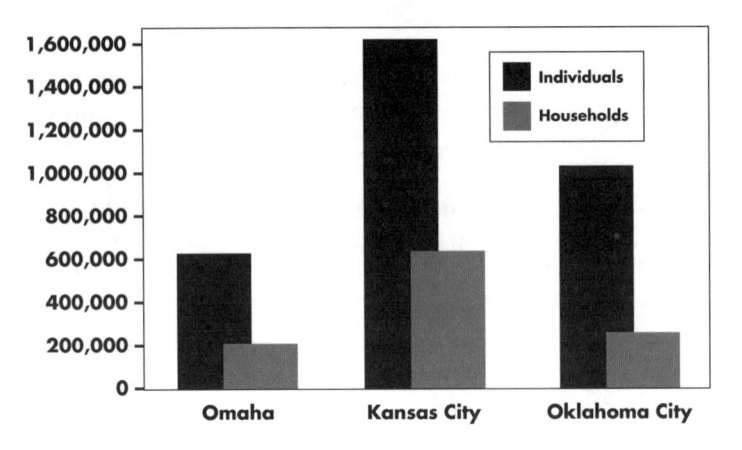

[Bar chart showing Individuals and Households for Omaha, Kansas City, and Oklahoma City]

Now I would like to take some time to look at some other statistics that suggest that financially, Omaha is an unusual place. To provide a basis for comparison, I have used figures from Kansas City and Oklahoma City, because these cities are also situated in the Midwest. All are similar in terms of demographics, climate, resources, and access to the coasts. Additionally, the cost of living indices for these cities are similar as is the similar makeup of their economies. The major difference lies in the size of their populations, but this is not necessarily a minus. If we choose, we can make population adjustments, and we have an opportunity to see where size might be a factor.

Let's begin with an overview of our three cities, starting with population figures. All the figures given are for the local SMSA or Standard Metropolitan Statistical Area. This represents not just the core city, but rather the metro area as defined by various governmental agencies.

As you can see, both of the cities I am using for comparison are larger than Omaha. Oklahoma City is 55% larger, and Kansas City is about 2-1/2 times larger.

Likewise, the breakdown of the economic base by type of business for the three cities is amazingly similar. The chart below summarizes the typical kinds of businesses found in this area.

**ECONOMIC BASE BY TYPE OF BUSINESS
AS A PERCENT OF THE TOTAL**

	Omaha	**Kansas City**	**Oklahoma City**
Agriculture	1.8	1.4	1.6
Construction	5.3	5.4	4.9
Manufacturing	11.6	13.1	11.75
Wholesale	5.2	5.5	4.7
Retail	18.5	16.8	17.2
Finances, Insurance	9.9	8.5	7.5
Services	34.6	32.2	34.3

(Figures do not round to 100 because small sectors are not included.)
(Source: The 1997 Census)

Agriculture plays only a small direct role in the economies of any of the three cities. In the case of Omaha, the indirect role of agriculture is significant. Many companies have agricultural concerns as their major customers. They process and transport the products that agriculture produces. Manufacturing represents only ten percent, the majority of which is not heavy industry. By far, the largest proportion is devoted to sales and services. Historically, the retail and service sectors can make use of a workforce with lower levels of technical skill, and can therefore pay their employees at the lower end of the wage spectrum,

However, let's take a look at the income figures for individuals. Median income represents the statistical point at which an equal number of people are above in income and an equal number are below. These figures, as gathered by the Census Bureau, are as follows:

APPENDIX

MEDIAN INCOME FIGURES
(Source: The 1997 Census)

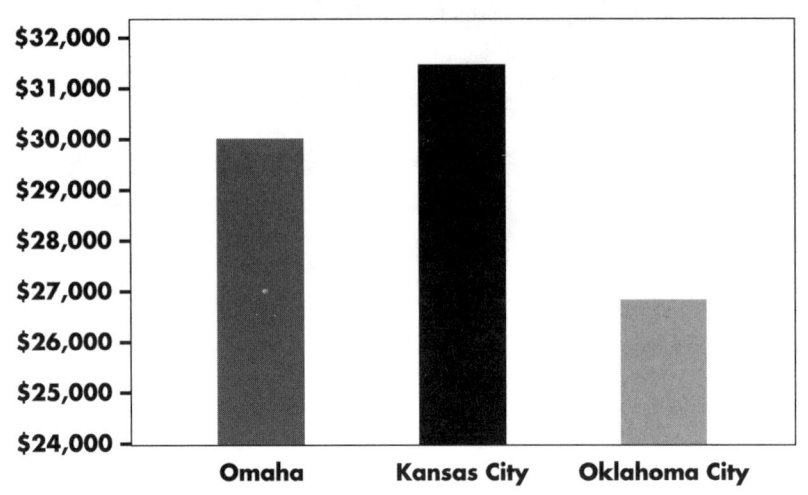

	Omaha	Kansas City	Oklahoma City
Median Income	~$30,000	~$31,500	~$26,750

The Census measures income in the traditional fashion: counting wages, salaries and government transfers, and is a gross, pretax dollar amount. From this perspective, Kansas City tops the list with a median income that is 5.9% higher than Omaha and 17.8% higher than Oklahoma City.

Were you to view Omaha from a conventional perspective, these are the results you would appear to get: Omaha residents have less spending power because of less income, on average, than people in similar cities. However, Omaha does not fit the conventional mold. A company called Sales and Marketing Management, a private corporation that compiles demographics which it sells to government agencies and corporations, developed an alternative way of measuring "income," called Effective Buying Income or EBI. EBI includes the income used in the Census calculation but also includes other sources of dollars not generated by wages and salaries.

These additional sources include self-employment income, interest, dividends and net rental income. From this gross figure, taxes are deducted to determine the actual buying power. This chart analyzes the effective buying power of people living in the three cities:

EFFECTIVE BUYING INCOME (EBI)
(Source: 1998 Sales and Marketing Management)

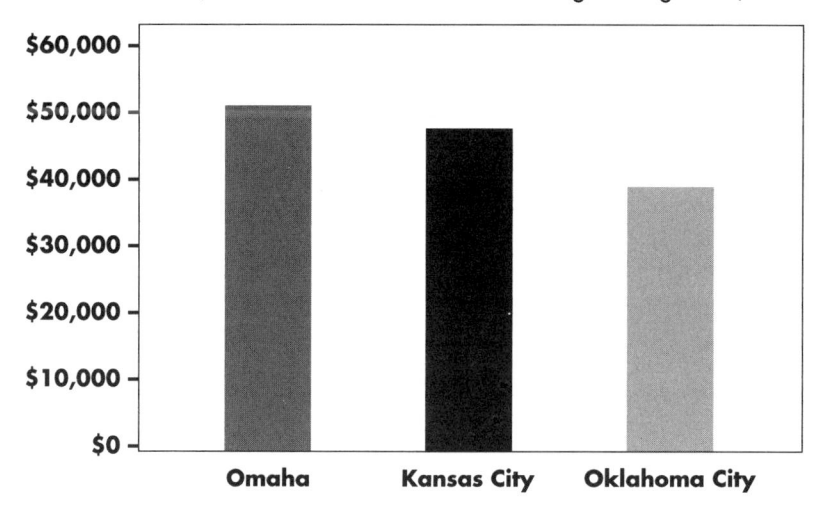

[Bar chart showing EBI values for Omaha (~$51,000), Kansas City (~$47,000), and Oklahoma City (~$39,000)]

These figures tell quite a different tale. All of the figures grow, but Omaha now jumps to the top of the list, with income growing a whopping 38.7%. Kansas City's income figure grew by only 20.8% and that of Oklahoma City by 16.4%. If you rank the cities by wages and salary, Omaha ranks in the middle. If you rank them by buying power, the Omaha figure increases dramatically. Why? The fact that many Omahans have additional sources of cash outside of their wages indicates that many own a significant amount of income-generating assets, which can include stocks, bonds, savings accounts, and investment or rental real estate.

To make a brief digression, let's look at Des Moines, Iowa, which is similar to Omaha, Kansas City, and Oklahoma City. However, it is smaller, with a population two-thirds that of Omaha. In Des Moines the median income figure for people is more like that of Kansas City and Oklahoma City rather than Omaha. In Des Moines the median is $31,182 and the EBI $38,013, a relationship almost identical to that of Kansas City.

Outside the Midwest, we find a number of cities with EBI figures greater than those of Omaha. These include Anchorage, Alaska, Honolulu, Hawaii, Bellevue, Washington and Newport Beach, California. The cost of living in Anchorage or Honolulu is dramatically higher than that of Omaha and the Midwest in general. Bellevue, Washington is home to many Microsoft people, and Newport Beach has strong connections with Hollywood. Both of these cities are examples of places where incomes are high. This does not necessarily indicate a high level of net worth. It is interesting to note that Omaha's EBI is 7.8% higher than Boca Raton, Florida and 4.3% higher than of Houston, Texas - two cities where you would expect to find a significant portion of the population with fairly high wage earners.

The significant number lies in the difference between the Census number and the EBI number. Here, Omaha stands nearly alone in the magnitude of gain from wages and salary to effective buying power. The next closest city is (surprise!) Lincoln, Nebraska, the state capital, which lies 60 miles southwest down Interstate 80 from Omaha, and is very similar to it, though smaller, with a population of not quite 200,000.

To demonstrate how this relates to the wealth base of Omaha, we can adjust the EBI figures for taxes. The Census numbers are before tax, and the EBI s are after tax. This allows us to make an apples-to-apples comparison.

PRE-TAX EBI MEDIAN INCOMES
(Source: 1998 Sales and Marketing Management)

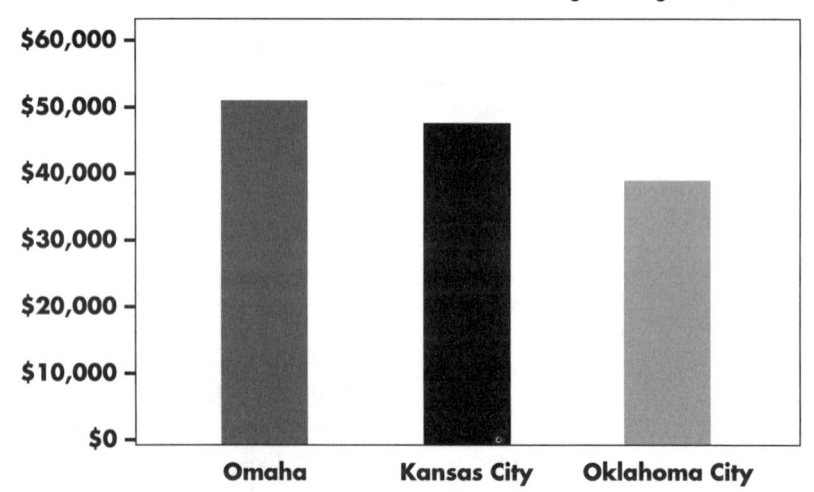

The spendable income of an average Omaha citizen is 73% when sources other than wages and salaries are included. An alternative way of expressing the same relationship is that 45 cents out of the average Omahan's spendable dollar comes from sources other than wages and salaries. For Kansas City, it is 31 cents, and for Oklahoma City, it is 30 cents.

A 15 cent difference may not seem like much until we take a look at the asset base this number implies. If the banks are paying 5%, and you earn dividends of $50, this implies that the amount for which you received dividends or interest income totals $1,000.

$$\$1,000 \times 5\% = \$50.00$$

So, if you earn $1,000 in dividends a year, by the same token, this implies that you have an account worth $20,000. Therefore, our 15 cent difference in the non-wage income between Omaha and Kansas City suggests that the asset base used to generate it is about 40.6% greater for Omaha and 86.9% larger for Oklahoma City. Again, the absolute figures are difficult to determine. But the relative size of the numbers are suggestive.

For the purpose of illustration, if you assume an overall 3% rate of return, then the average asset base for the three cities would be as follows:

PRE-TAX EBI MEDIAN INCOMES
(Source: 1998 Sales and Marketing Management)

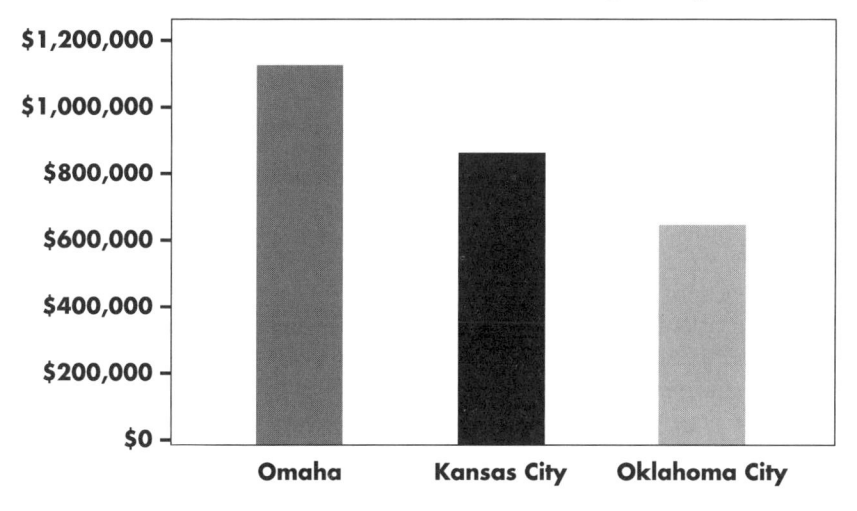

[Bar chart showing approximate values: Omaha ~$1,130,000; Kansas City ~$860,000; Oklahoma City ~$650,000]

If you change the rate of return, the absolute value of these figures will change, but the percentages remain the same.

One other measure indicating an above-average concentration of wealth is found in the relative size of the broker population of our peer cities. City-specific figures are available on the number of people who hold a Series 7 license with the National Association of Securities Dealers. This number will include full-service brokers, their assistants, management officials of the firm, and often some people who work in various accounting positions. In order to derive a reasonable figure for full-service brokers per city, I took the national ratios and applied them to the figures for our respective cities. These figures were then broken down on a per capita basis.

APPENDIX

NUMBER OF PEOPLE PER BROKER

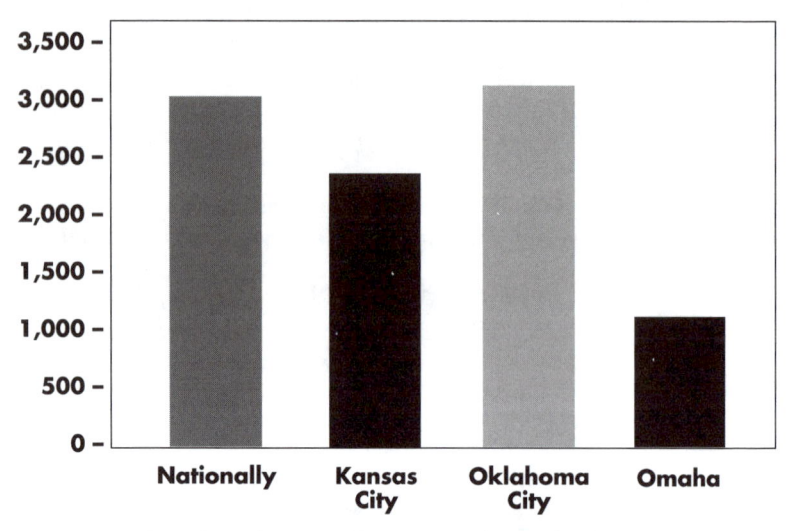

| Nationally | Kansas City | Oklahoma City | Omaha |

To translate this, there are fewer people per broker in Omaha! The number indicates that in Kansas City, one broker may need to take care of 2,987 people. In Oklahoma City, one broker may take care of 3,061. While in Omaha, one broker need take care of only 1,058 people. Why is this important? These figures are revealing, because in order for brokers to be profitable, they need to have a reasonable number of dollars under their management. I cannot give you an exact figure, but we can still draw reasonable conclusions about the average per capita worth of brokerage accounts for our comparison group. More brokers are serving fewer customers in Omaha because they can make a living doing it. Their small but affluent customer base is sufficient to support them and a host of others like them.

For example, if you assume that the average broker had $50 million under management and multiplied that by the number of brokers per city, you could estimate cities' gross publicly traded net worth. Dividing that figure by the population gives you a per capita net worth. Here are the figures for our peer group:

PER CAPITA NET WORTH

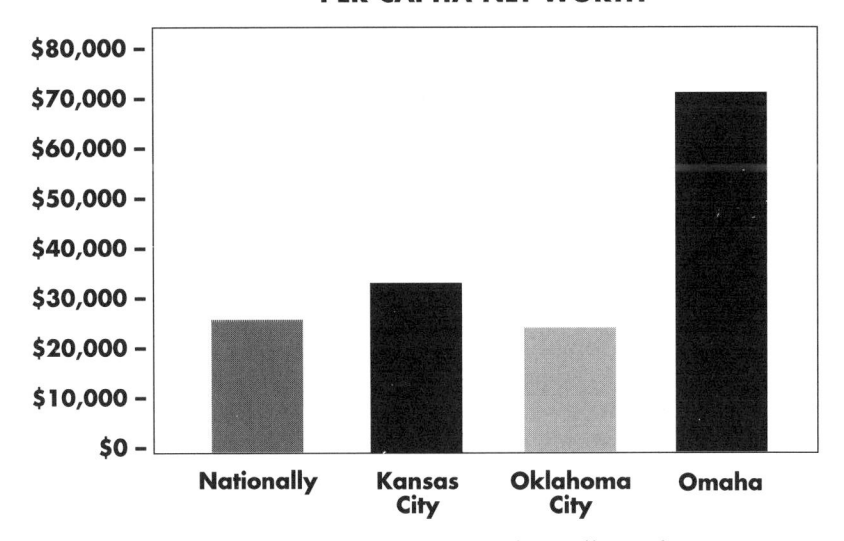

$80,000	
$70,000	
$60,000	
$50,000	
$40,000	
$30,000	
$20,000	
$10,000	
$0	

Nationally   Kansas City   Oklahoma City   Omaha

Again, these are not absolute figures. They tell us relative sizes. In line with everything we have seen so far, it appears that the average Omaha brokerage account is about 3 times larger than that of its peers in similar Midwestern cities.

So far, I have found no single cause for this phenomenon. However, there is an abundance of data suggesting a possible reason. If you review Omaha from an "income perspective," you may have an impression that it is a ho-hum, ordinary kind of place. However, if you look at it from a perspective of "net worth" a very different picture of wealth begins to emerge. It appears that there are more people in Omaha with more spending power than there are in similar places elsewhere. The question is why – or how this happened. Let's look at a small subgroup of these affluent people in Omaha. Many people nowadays can be called "millionaires" but only a few might be categorized as "mega-millionaires" with assets of $100, $200, $300, million or more.

My figures for the number of Omaha mega-millionaires are derived from a variety of sources. Proxy statements from various companies are the most accurate source. By law, a company's proxy statement contains an accounting of all shares held by the members of the board of directors and the senior officers. In addition, I have used earnings estimates of privately held companies as a method of valuing those assets. I also have taken articles from local and national media sources for other estimates. In some cases, I identified the price and date of a company's sale, and made projections of the possible current net worth of those assets, assuming they have not been spent or gifted away.

APPENDIX

All of this results in a list of individuals and families who I am fairly certain meet the criteria for being mega-millionaires. To corroborate my figures, I showed them to a wide number of other financial professionals in Omaha. They tended to confirm my findings and several even felt I might be a bit low in my estimates in several categories.

Let's begin with the really rich, starting at the top with billionaires. Omaha has two individuals who are generally accepted as being members of this elite club, Warren Buffett and Walter Scott. The actual figure lies between five and eight. To put this group in perspective, let's take a look at *Forbes* Magazine's "List of the 400 Richest People in America." *Forbes* lists 235 billionaires for the entire nation. That's 1 billionaire for every 1,191,489 people. (The same measure for Omaha is about 1 billionaire per 136,000 people!)

Since the inception of *Forbes'* 400 List in 1983, the cutoff figure has steadily climbed. It now stands at $500 million. How does Omaha stack up in the lofty $500 million area? On the *Forbes'* list, Omaha has two entries (Buffett and Scott); Kansas City, two; and Oklahoma City, one. But, there are probably many, many more from Omaha with assets in the $500 million to billion range. *Forbes'* national figure for persons in this category is 165. But since they missed all those in Omaha, I am certain that the *Forbes'* number significantly underrepresented reality. My research suggest that there may be as many as 120 families living in Omaha with a net worth over $100 million.

Now lets look at the next level down, those millionaires who perhaps fall into the $50 million-plus category. An IRS study in 1997 estimates that there were 8,600 in this category nationally. Using this figure as a benchmark, we would expect Omaha to have 20 in this category. Our best estimate is there are probably 300 to 350 Omaha residents in the $50 million to $100 million range. In this category, we begin to run into a higher percentage of privately held companies than we experienced in the $100+ million group, so a precise figure is more difficult to obtain. (One fascinating subgroup is a group of people who own a large number of fast food franchises. Seven entrepreneurs in Omaha own a large number of franchises, including Burger King, Godfather's Pizza, and McDonald's.)

Finally, let's look at the regular millionaires in Omaha. The IRS figure would put Omaha as having 3,300. My best estimate is that the actual number lies closer to 15,000. The primary reason for this discrepancy lies in the number of Omaha companies who have rewarded their employees with stock in their company. And as I will show, the value of these companies exceeds that of their peer groups and the national average as well.

Let's turn our focus to the publicly traded companies created by these millionaires. Because they are publicly traded, we can derive fairly accurate measures of their overall worth. Next, how much of the net worth of these companies can we attribute to local ownership? Again, because publicly traded companies have high disclosure requirements we are able to get fairly accurate figures from the proxy statements of all the companies that list the shares owned by senior officers and members of the Board of Directors.

PERCENT OF LOCAL OWNERSHIP

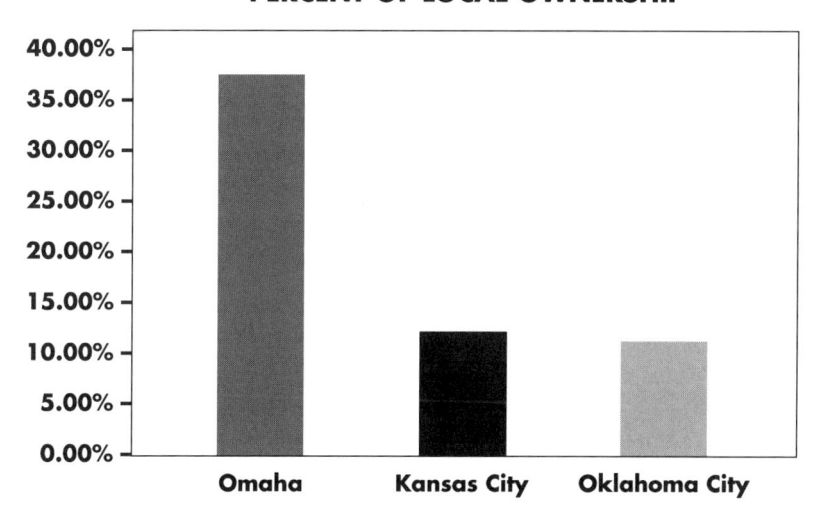

City	Percent
Omaha	~37.5%
Kansas City	~12%
Oklahoma City	~11%

As you can see, Omaha companies have a significantly higher level of ownership by the officers of the company. We will revisit these numbers when we discuss what the people in Omaha do in order to bring about these unusual results.

There is another measure to support this observation. For the past ten years a brokerage firm headquartered in Omaha has constructed an index of Nebraska companies that tracks companies headquartered in Nebraska. True, it is not an exclusively Nebraska index, but I think it can be used, with some caveats, to compare the market performance of the Omaha companies to the national numbers. There are 33 companies in the total. Of these, 21 are from Omaha. Of the total market represented by the Nebraska Index, over 85% comes from Omaha. So let's see how the Nebraska Companies compare to two of the best-known stock indexes.

APPENDIX

PERCENT GROWTH IN 1989 TO 1999
(Courtesy of Kirkpatrick Pettis Research)

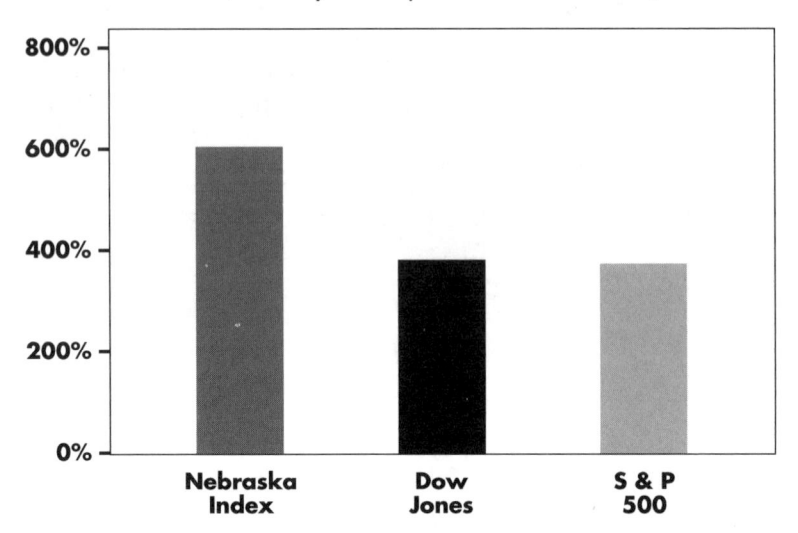

	Nebraska Index	Dow Jones	S & P 500
Growth	~600%	~380%	~370%

The market value of Nebraska companies has grown at a rate that is almost twice that of the Dow and S & P. Oklahoma City does not have a local stock index, but one does exist for Kansas City.

Thus, Omaha compares even more favorably against Kansas City than the national averages.

PERCENT GROWTH IN 1989 TO 1999
(Courtesy of Bloomberg News Service)

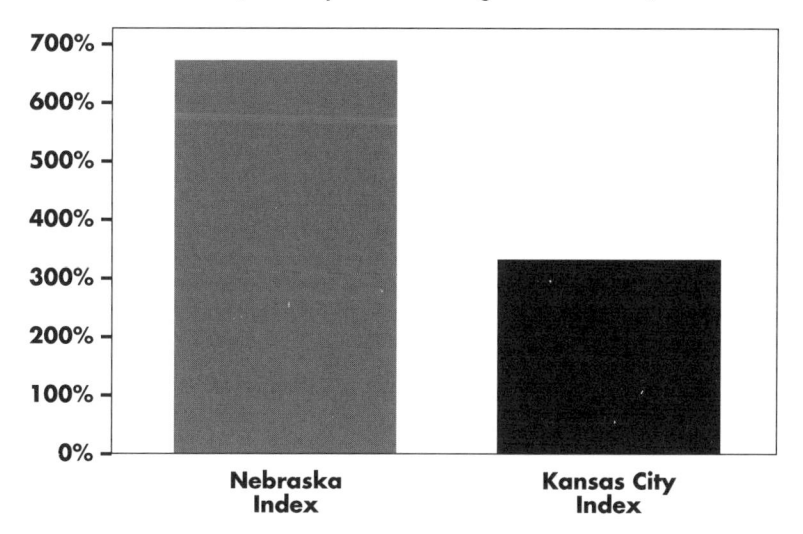

Taken at face value, these results are interesting, but when these relatively small differences in the growth rates of these companies are compounded over time, the results are dramatic.

Consider the following: if you were to invest $10,000 in a company and had the results listed on page 153, the amount you would have after 25 years would be as follows:

COMPOUNDING RESULTS AFTER 25 YEARS OF A $10,000 INVESTMENT

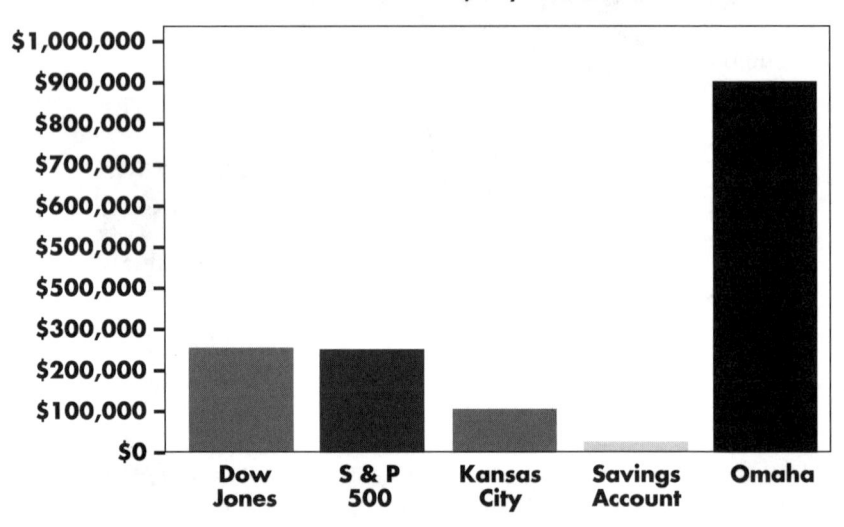

Dow Jones	S & P 500	Kansas City	Savings Account	Omaha
~$250,000	~$250,000	~$100,000	~$20,000	~$900,000

This gives us significant insight into why Omaha has such a high concentration of multi- and mega-millionaires. It is because of the quality of its companies. By quality, I mean the ability to make the *value* of the company grow at above average rates for long periods of time.

In closing, I would like to state that there is a subjective element to the statistics I have just presented. The task of comparing Omaha to the nation in all these statistical categories is frankly overwhelming. So I would be the first to admit that my case is not iron clad. But, I hope that you have been convinced that Omaha shows signs of having a fairly unique economic community.